Handbook for Teaching Japanese-Speaking Students

Developed by the
Bilingual Education Office
California State Department of Education

Publishing Information

This handbook was funded in part with funds from the Office of Bilingual Education and Minority Language Affairs and the Office of Equal Educational Opportunity Programs, U.S. Department of Education. The opinions expressed herein do not, however, necessarily reflect the position or policy of the U.S. Department of Education, and no official endorsement by the U.S. Department of Education should be inferred. The document was developed by the Bilingual Education Office, California State Department of Education. The final draft of the manuscript was edited by Mirko Strazicich of the Bureau of Publications, working in cooperation with Daniel D. Holt of the Bilingual Education Office. The handbook was prepared for photo-offset production by the staff of the Bureau of Publications, with artwork by Cheryl Shawver McDonald and Paul Lee. The document was published by the Department; printed by the Office of State Printing; and distributed under the provisions of the Library Distribution Act and *Government Code* Section 11096.

California State Department of Education

Copies of this handbook are available for $4.50 each, plus sales tax for California residents, from Publications Sales, P.O. Box 271, Sacramento, CA 95802-0271.

A list of other publications available from the Department of Education is shown on page 123.

ISBN 0-8011-0680-X

Contents

Page

Foreword... v
Preface... vii
Acknowledgments...................................... ix
Note to Readers...................................... xi

Chapter I. Background of Japanese-Speaking People
    in California...................................... 1
    Overview of the Japanese Language Group............... 1
    History of Japanese Immigration....................... 2
    Reasons for Japanese Immigration...................... 7
    Location of Japanese Residents in the U.S............... 8
    Japanese Residing in Other Countries................... 9
    Quality of Education in Japan......................... 9
    Role of the Immigrant as Teacher or Tutor 12
    Attitudes of Japanese Parents......................... 13

Chapter II. Historical and Sociocultural Factors Concerning
    the Japanese Language.............................. 15
    Language Education in Japan.......................... 15
    Attitudes Toward Oral Skills.......................... 18
    Learning English in Japan............................ 21
    Using English in Japan............................... 22
    Language Education in California....................... 23

Chapter III. Linguistic Characteristics of the Japanese Language 29
    Origin of the Japanese Language....................... 29
    Characteristics of Japanese Written Language............ 39
    Introduction of the Language Systems................... 44
    Interrelationship Between Language and Culture.......... 45
    Nonverbal Behaviors That Affect Learning.............. 49

Chapter IV. Recommended Instructional and Curricular
    Strategies for Japanese Language Development.......... 53
    Readiness Skills..................................... 54
    Oral Language Skills................................. 58
    Literacy Development in English....................... 58
    Planning a Japanese Reading Program................... 60
    Methods for Teaching Reading in Japanese.............. 62
    Methods for Teaching Writing in Japanese.............. 69

Introduction of Oral English Instruction................... 71
Submersion Environments.............................. 72
Reading in Two Languages............................. 74
Summarizing the Discussion on Strategies................ 77

Glossary... 78
Bibliography... 84

Selected References................................. 84
Suggested Readings................................. 87

Appendix A. Districts Ranked by Enrollment of Limited-English-
            Proficient Students Who Speak Japanese...... 90
Appendix B. Educational Resources....................... 92
Appendix C. Course of Study for Japanese Language
            in Elementary Schools in Japan............. 101
Appendix D. Japanese Holidays, Ceremonies, and Festivals.... 119

List of Tables and Figures

Table   *Page*
  1 Immigration into the United States
     from Japan, 1861—1968......................... 6

Figure
  1 A page from a student's textbook, illustrating the use
     of different Japanese writing systems............... 43
  2 Workbook exercises in writing *hiragana* and *kanji*....... 70
  3 A typical entry in a children's *kanji* dictionary.......... 71

Foreword

During the 1986-87 school year, 10,599 students in California were reported to be using Japanese as their primary home language. Approximately 3,950 of these students were identified as limited-English proficient (LEP). This publication, *A Handbook for Teaching Japanese-Speaking Students,* was developed to help educators provide the best educational opportunities for Japanese-speaking students.

What is especially important is that teachers and administrators have adequate knowledge of Japanese students' language and cultural background. This knowledge, research has shown, has a significant influence on the scholastic performance of language minority students. With the information provided in this handbook, school district personnel should be able to design and implement effective instructional programs that address the specific needs of Japanese-speaking students.

Included in the handbook is information on the unique historical, sociocultural, and linguistic characteristics of Japanese-speaking students. The handbook also provides information about educational resources, such as community organizations, public agencies, and classroom instructional materials. We in the Department are pleased to be involved in the development of this handbook. We believe that it and handbooks for other language groups will make an important contribution to the improvement of educational services for language minority students.

Bill Honig

Superintendent of Public Instruction

Preface

This handbook was developed as part of the Asian and Minority Language Group Project in the Bilingual Education Office, California State Department of Education. The project was designed to assist school districts in providing effective bilingual education services to language minority students, and the Project Team identified as its first major activity the development of handbooks for a number of Asian and minority language groups.

The purpose of the handbooks is to assist school personnel in understanding selected Asian and minority language groups. The handbooks have been designed for use by bilingual education specialists as well as administrators and teachers who have more general responsibilities for the education of language minority students.

Chapters I and II of this handbook address general background factors regarding the Japanese-speaking language groups: immigration history, educational background, and sociocultural factors. Chapters III and IV contain specific information regarding the Japanese language and appropriate program offerings that will promote the academic achievement of Japanese-speaking students.

This handbook is complemented by other publications developed by the Bilingual Education Office, including *Schooling and Language Minority Students: A Theoretical Framework,*[1] which provides extensive information regarding bilingual education theory and practice. It also outlines the basic principles underlying successful bilingual education programs and suggests a variety of implementation strategies.

The analyses and illustrations in the *Theoretical Framework* are not specific to particular language groups. Rather, the *Theoretical Framework* provides a way of conceptualizing and organizing appropriate program services based on program goals, available resources, community background factors, and student characteristics.

The handbook and others developed as part of the Asian and Minority Language Group Project are designed to assist school district personnel in better understanding specific Asian and minority language group communities and individual students who come from

---

[1]Information regarding this publication is available from the Evaluation, Dissemination, and Assessment Center, California State University, Los Angeles, 5151 State University Drive, Los Angeles, CA 90032. The Center also has handbooks on Vietnamese-speaking and Korean-speaking students.

these communities.[2] We believe that by using this handbook in conjunction with the *Theoretical Framework*, school personnel should be able to develop program services that are appropriately suited to the needs of individual Japanese-speaking students.

The Asian and Minority Language Group Project Team of the Bilingual Education Office began development of this handbook in January, 1980. It went through several drafts and was reviewed by teachers, linguists, and members of the language group community before publication. Every effort has been made to create a handbook that would be useful to educators who are responsible for the education of Asian and minority groups.

An ad hoc committee representing 13 different language groups identified five key areas where information would be useful to school districts. Each of the handbooks addresses these areas. The first two chapters of the handbook are designed to provide a general understanding of the social and educational background of the language group and of its history of immigration to the United States. The final two chapters on linguistics and program development are designed for bilingual educators who are developing appropriate curriculum and instruction for language minority students. The appendixes provide a variety of available resources for the education of students of the language group.

In spite of extensive work done by many individuals on the handbook, it should be regarded as a first edition. As time and resources permit, efforts will be made to refine it. It is difficult in one volume to depict the uniqueness and heterogeneity that characterize the language group. The reader should recognize that any language group is complex and diverse, with individual members and generations having a variety of needs and characteristics based on different experiences in America and in their native countries.

This handbook represents an initial attempt to describe generally the needs and characteristics of the language minority groups. Much more research and developmental work needs to be done by all who are responsible for ensuring the successful adaptation to America by minority language groups.

JAMES R. SMITH
Director, Curriculum
and Instructional Leadership Branch

RAMIRO D. REYES
Director, Categorical Support
Programs Division

LEO LOPEZ
Manager, Bilingual
Education Office

---

[2]Handbooks on Cantonese-speaking, Pilipino-speaking, and Portuguese-speaking students are available from Bureau of Publications Sales, California State Department of Education, P.O. Box 271, Sacramento, CA 95802-0271 (phone: 916-445-1260).

Acknowledgments

The California State Department of Education wishes to recognize the many individuals who assisted in completing this handbook. The facilitator, Mary G. McDonald, former Director of the BABEL LAU Center, Oakland, worked closely with the project team in keeping the handbook on schedule and in making revisions to the drafts. As a result of her extensive study of the language and culture of Japan, Ms. McDonald was able to lead the development of the handbook with competence and dedication.

Ms. McDonald collaborated with the language group representatives—Mieko S. Han, Institute for Intercultural Studies, Los Angeles, and Kathy Reyes, formerly with San Francisco Unified School District—in writing sections of the handbook and doing needed research. George Kiriyama, Los Angeles Unified School District, and Kikuko Nishi, Torrance Unified School District, reviewed the final manuscript and provided invaluable suggestions. Space does not permit listing the many interested members of the language group community and the wider public who suggested improvements for various drafts.

This handbook and others were developed as part of the Asian and Minority Language Group Project. The previously published handbooks were for students who speak Vietnamese, Korean, Portuguese, Cantonese, and Pilipino. The project was originally designed by a team of consultants from the Bilingual Education Office: David P. Dolson, Daniel D. Holt, Chong K. Park, and Van Le. The project received administrative support from Leo Lopez, Manager, and Sarah Gomez, Assistant Manager, Bilingual Education Office.

The Department acknowledges the following specialists who assisted the writers at the beginning of the project in May, 1980: Eleanor W. Thonis, Wheatland Elementary School District; Benjamin K. T'sou, City Polytechnic College of Hong Kong; and Lily Wong-Fillmore, University of California, Berkeley. Special thanks is also extended to Etsuko Wakayama, Dean, Sakura Gakuen Japanese School, for checking the accuracy of the Japanese characters.

Although many individuals contributed to each handbook, final responsibility rests with the Bilingual Education Office, California State Department of Education.

DANIEL D. HOLT
Asian and Minority Language
Group Project Team Leader

Note to Readers

This handbook is designed for use by administrators, teachers, and other instructional personnel. The contents of the handbook may help the user in many different ways.

Chapter I. Background of Japanese-Speaking People in California

Material in this chapter should help school personnel to:

1. Develop positive attitudes toward the Japanese language group by understanding general factors related to the group's experience in California.
2. Develop continuity in the immigrating students' education by realizing various aspects of their socioeducational experiences in the native country.
3. Improve parent and community participation by knowing more about the group's attitudes toward schooling.
4. Develop staff recruitment strategies by understanding the educational background of the immigrating adults.

Chapter II. Historical and Sociocultural Factors Concerning the Japanese Language

Material in this chapter should help school personnel to:

1. Develop effective curricular and instructional approaches by understanding how educators in the native country deal with literacy and language arts.
2. Improve English instruction by understanding what contact, if any, students have had with English in the native country.
3. Promote Japanese language development by knowing how the Japanese language is reinforced in the home and community in California.
4. Improve academic performance by understanding the role of the Japanese language in formal schooling contexts.

Chapter III. Linguistic Characteristics of the Japanese Language

Material in this chapter should help school personnel to:

1. Create Japanese language development activities by knowing more about the linguistic aspects of the language.
2. Improve English language instruction by understanding some of the similarities and differences between English and the Japanese language.

Chapter IV. Recommended Instructional and Curricular Strategies for Japanese Language Development

Material in this chapter should help school personnel to:

1. Improve Japanese language and English instruction by better understanding the theoretical bases for bilingual instruction.
2. Improve Japanese language and English instruction by realizing how to manage the student's contact in the United States with both languages in the school and community.
3. Improve academic performance by understanding the role of the Japanese language in formal schooling contexts.

Glossary, Bibliography, and Appendixes

The material in the glossary, bibliography, and appendixes should help the school staff to:

1. Select materials necessary for language arts and other curricular areas.
2. Develop constructive relationships with community organizations and media services related to curriculum and instruction.
3. Create liaison with other districts in California by knowing where students of the Japanese language group are concentrated.
4. Use terms that are associated with the Japanese language group and educational services to support it.

Chapter I

Background of Japanese-Speaking People in California

The century spanning the years between the 1880s and the present has encompassed many changes within both Japan and the United States and in the relations between the two countries. All of these changes have influenced the numbers, the motivations, and the characteristics of Japanese people coming to make a home in California. The long history of Japanese immigration to America requires two main distinctions when discussing the Japanese language group. First, the nationality of any member of this group might be either American or Japanese. Second, the native language of any person of this group might be English or Japanese.

Overview of the Japanese Language Group

The distinction between the generations of Japanese Americans and Japanese nationals is often made through the following Japanese terms:

- *Issei* are literally first-generation Japanese Americans. Most of these men and women immigrated to the United States with the thought of eventually returning to Japan, but they stayed for various reasons to raise their families here. Many *issei* who were pioneer immigrants from Japan in the early 1900s are now quite elderly.

- *Nisei* are literally second-generation Japanese Americans. They were born in this country of *issei* parents. *Nisei* are now over fifty years of age and working in all occupations.

- *Sansei* and *yonsei* are third-generation and fourth-generation Japanese Americans. Members of these younger generations may or may not have learned to speak Japanese at home, but usually they have participated in organizations and annual events associated with Japanese-American culture. As with all other Americans, *sansei* and *yonsei* vary widely in their familiarity with the language and culture of modern Japan.

- *Shōsha* families are Japanese citizens who are living in the United States in connection with their employment in a Japanese business enterprise. (*Shōsha* is the Japanese word for company.)

1

The growth of joint Japanese-American ventures in trade, manufacturing, and banking has brought increasing numbers of Japanese families on temporary assignment—usually two to five years—to overseas offices in California.

Of course, many other individuals of Japanese backgrounds do not fit into any of the categories above, such as Japanese students or visiting scholars in California universities or Japanese-born women who have married American husbands and now live permanently in this country. Furthermore, many youngsters of the Japanese language group in our schools have parents of two different backgrounds.

Given this diversity of generations and nationalities, the "Japanese language group" actually includes people with a great range of proficiencies in both Japanese and English. Some children hear both Japanese and English at home; and in some cases, a third language. Chances are that any student who comes to a California public school as a speaker of Japanese with limited-English proficiency was either born in Japan or has at least one Japanese-born parent.

History of Japanese Immigration

Modern exchange between Japan and the United States began in the 1850s and 1860s with a new and energetic trans-Pacific awareness on the part of both Japanese and Americans. When three American "black ships" sailed into Tokyo Bay in July, 1853, more than 250 years of deliberate Japanese isolation from the outside world was broken. A new and tenuous link was forged between two worlds, each in the midst of its own great social change.

The official interests of the United States at that time were to establish favorable commercial trade agreements with Japan and to secure assistance and provisions for American ships stopping on Japanese shores. Already accustomed to contracting Chinese laborers from the ports of China, American entrepreneurs sought other laborers from Japan to work in sugarcane fields of Hawaii and the booming agricultural regions of California (Treat, 1963).

While American petitioners waited on Japanese shores through the 1850s and 1860s for the Japanese to sign trade agreements, an all-encompassing civil revolution was taking place within Japan. Much of Japan's internal unrest pivoted on the question of Japan's future relations with the other nations of the world. Many Japanese were afraid of the kind of humiliation that their great neighbor China had suffered at the hands of the English; however, the Japanese realized that their defenses were no match for the gunboats of the Americans. Reminded by Commodore Matthew Perry that the United States had recently won a war against Mexico and had annexed former Mexican territory (Treat, 1963), the Japanese Shogunate had little choice but to enter into "diplomatic relations" with the Americans. This move proved highly controversial within Japan, fueling the internal criticism of the government and furthering a new nationalistic fervor for a revitalized Japan that could hold its own among world powers (Jansen, 1982).

The centralized power of the Shogun began to crumble in the 1860s as support grew for the restoration of the long-cloistered imperial family as the real head of government. Long-standing political rivalry among various Japanese clans broke into open civil war over this issue, leading to the eventual dissolution of the Shogunate and the rise in 1868 of the young, capable Emperor Meiji to the leadership of a new form of government. With the fall of many old feudal institutions and lines of authority, many families' rank, holdings, and access to political influence were completely altered during the 1860s. A new sense of personal mobility was awakened with the changes in the social order (Jansen, 1982).

Supporters of the imperial restoration had won their campaign on a wave of antiforeign nationalism, but the new government soon looked abroad for models of development that Japanese modernization could follow. Emperor Meiji was determined that his island nation would replicate the best of Western technology, government, defense, transportation, and education. In the Charter Oath of April 6, 1868, the Emperor decreed:

Knowledge shall be sought throughout the world, so that the foundations of the Empire may be strengthen. (Ichihashi, 1969)

In 1871 the Emperor further revealed his strategy for modernization:

During youthtime it is positively necessary to view foreign countries, so as to become enlightened as to the ideas of the world; and boys as well as girls, who will themselves become men and women, should be allowed to go abroad, and my country will benefit by their knowledge so acquired. (Ichihashi, 1969)

By ending the total ban on foreign travel that had encompassed Japan for hundreds of years, the Emperor launched a deliberate program to educate young people and government officials in the ways of industrialized nations, including the United States. Beginning in 1868, Japan sponsored foreign tours for educational purposes, and the first records of Japanese in the United States describe the activities of these official delegations of visitors and students.

Still, however, Japan was reluctant to allow the legal emigration of its citizens to foreign countries to work and live. The bitter experiences of two groups of Japanese workers who were spirited out of Japan without government permission reinforced the government's hesitation to allow the emigration of laborers. The first episode involved a shipload of Japanese—141 men, six women, and one child—who were brought to Hawaii in 1868 as contract laborers (Daniels, 1968). These individuals, who were recruited off the streets of Yokohama during the midst of the civil strife, had no farming experience. Thus, they had difficulty adjusting to life as plantation workers in Hawaii. The Japanese government was distressed by the unhappy reports of the laborers and of their employers and so reaffirmed its refusal to issue passports to Japanese for purposes of working abroad.

Nevertheless, a second group of emigrants without proper passports left Japan in 1869 for California to establish the first Japanese settlement in the United States. These 26 men and women of the Aizu-Wakamatsu region of Japan had sided with the Shogun's resistance to the imperial forces. After the demise of the Shogunate, they were attracted to commercial prospects in a new land. They intended to establish a tea- and silk-producing colony at Gold Hill, El Dorado County, California, under the leadership of a German-born businessman. For reasons still not clearly known, however, this "Aizu-Wakamatsu Colony" ended in failure after only two years.

The two unsuccessful experiences increased Japan's wariness of sending workers abroad under contract with foreigners. Besides, Japan was engaged in efforts to populate its northernmost island of Hokkaido. Between 1869 and 1884, more than 100,000 Japanese moved to new settlements in Hokkaido (Daniels, 1968). By 1884, however, a period of severe economic distress among small farmers all over Japan (Conroy, 1973) coincided with intensified solicitations by the Hawaiian sugar industry and United States labor contractors. The American anti-Chinese Restriction Act of 1882 had barred the further admission of Chinese laborers, thus creating severe labor shortages in the western states and renewing American pressure on the Japanese government to allow its citizens to work abroad. Yielding to both internal and external pressures, the Japanese government finally relaxed its position and legalized emigration in 1886.

Thus, in 1884 a stream of Japanese immigrants began arriving in Hawaii and California for purposes of living and working as laborers. Many immigrants came under contract with agricultural or food-processing employers. Contracts typically lasted for three years and guaranteed each worker $9 a month with food or $15 a month without food (Ichihashi, 1969). Most of the young Japanese men who signed such contracts had every intention of saving their salaries and returning to Japan with a fortune of perhaps $200.

Between 1884 and 1907 thousands of young Japanese workers under such contracts arrived in California and Hawaii. Of course, when Hawaii became a United States Territory in 1900, Japanese who were already in Hawaii could proceed to California without further immigration formalities, so immigration figures from the early years of this century may not be precise. Some Japanese remained in the United States even after their contracts expired, continuing to work as free laborers, as tenant farmers, or in small service enterprises of their own. The modest success of small independent Japanese farmers and businessmen soon became the focus of vehement anti-Asian sentiments, seen earlier in anti-Chinese movements, especially in California. In 1907 the United States government, responding to increasing threats of violence against the Japanese in California, concluded a "gentlemen's agreement" with Japan. Under this agreement Japan promised to send no more unskilled laborers to the United States in exchange for respectful treatment of Japanese citizens in this country. Facing a hostile social and economic environment in California, many Japanese workers fulfilled their original intention of returning to Japan. In the years between 1908 and 1913, the number of Japanese departing from the United States, 31,777, exceeded the number of Japanese admitted, 30,985 (Millis, 1979). But for many Japanese, the hostile economic environment meant precisely that their intentions of returning to Japan could *not* be realized (Wilson and Hosokawa, 1982). The Japanese men and women who remained in California and Hawaii became the original first generation of Japanese Americans.

The Gentlemen's Agreement of 1907 did not totally seal off the immigration of Japanese to the West Coast, but it did decrease the numbers that entered. Nor did the Gentlemen's Agreement quell the growing anti-Japanese sentiment directed at the increasing numbers of Japanese who had become independent farmers in California. The California Alien Land Law of 1913 prevented Japanese immigrants from owning land and limited leases of land to aliens to three years. The purpose behind this discriminatory law was to drive the Japanese out of agriculture and eventually out of California.

By 1924 agitation against the Japanese was so intense—both in urban and rural settings throughout the western states—that the Oriental Exclusion Act, which entirely shut off immigration from all Asian countries, was passed by Congress. Inasmuch as the Chinese had not been admitted since 1882, the Oriental Exclusion Act of 1924 was clearly intended for the Japanese. Table 1 illustrates the precipitous drop in Japanese immigration following the Exclusion Act of the mid-1920s.

Despite the 1924 Exclusion Act, by 1940 some 126,000 Japanese and Japanese Americans lived in the continental United States. Anti-Japanese sentiments continued to be spread by the media and expressed by labor leaders, industrialists, and politicians throughout

5

Table 1

Immigration into the United States from Japan, 1861—1968

Period	Number of immigrants
1861—1870	186
1871—1880	149
1881—1890	2,270
1891—1900	25,942
1901—1910	129,797
1911—1920	83,837
1921—1930	33,462
1931—1940	1,948
1941—1950	1,555
1951—1960	46,250
1961	4,490
1962	4,054
1963	4,147
1964	3,774
1965	3,294
1966	3,468
1967	4,125
1968	3,810

TOTAL 356,558

Source: Wilson and Hosokawa, 1982.

the 1920s and 1930s. Thus, at the outbreak of America's involvement in World War II in December, 1941, the ethnic Japanese in the United States were ready targets for removal from their homes, land, and property along the West Coast. In 1942 the federal government summarily ordered some 110,000 "persons of Japanese ancestry," of whom 75,000 were American citizens by birth, out of their homes in the western states and transported them to ten internment camps for the duration of World War II.

In 1952, seven years after the end of the war, the Japanese immigrants finally became eligible for United States citizenship through the passage of the McCarren-Walter Act. This law also allowed immigration of Japanese to resume and made Japanese nationals eligible for the status of "permanent residents." Although the number of immigrants to be accepted each year was limited to a quota of 180 persons, the law provided also for the entry of persons with special skills and of additional family members of Japanese already in this country. The greatest significance of the McCarren-Walter Act is that it allowed the first generation of Japanese immigrants, the *issei,* to finally become full-fledged citizens of their adopted country.

In 1965 an amendment to the McCarren-Walter Act was enacted. By abolishing the quota system applied to each country and greatly liberalizing American immigration policy, this new legislation opened the way for tens of thousands of immigrants from all over the world to enter the United States each year. However, unlike some other Asian nations, the level of immigration from Japan did not change. Since the enactment of the 1965 amendment, Japanese immigration to the United States has remained low, from 3,000 to 4,000 persons per year. This trend attests to the relative social and economic stability enjoyed in Japan in recent years, which precludes most Japanese from uprooting themselves to begin a new life in America.

As a result of the new prosperity of Japan's commercial and industrial interests, however, California has received many Japanese businessmen and their families during the 1970s and 1980s. Such families spend from two to five years on assignment with a California branch of their Japan-based companies. These individuals are not counted as immigrants in official statistics, because they are in the United States on temporary visas.

Reasons for Japanese Immigration

The majority of immigrants from Japan to America have come in response to specific work-related opportunities. Most have held in mind (at least initially) the possibility of eventually returning to Japan. Around the turn of the century, when many social and economic stresses disrupted their traditional agricultural livelihood, many young Japanese were enticed by emigration companies to seek employment opportunities in California. As discussed earlier in the section on the history of Japanese immigration, some saw this as a chance to earn a small nest egg for a fresh start in Japan. Neither religion nor politics motivated most Japanese immigrants, although some men between the ages of twenty and thirty-seven may have been happy to avoid military conscription in Japan in the early decades of this century (Wilson and Hosokawa, 1982). A common turning point for many early immigrants in their decision to remain in California was the birth of children. Once young *issei* couples began to raise their families here, they chose to remain in the land that was their children's home.

Today, both schooling and commercial assignments continue to bring many Japanese to spend several years in California. Few Japanese families without affiliation to a company or a university arrive here now. The husband frequently has a secure job in the intellectual or managerial strata of Japanese society, so the family is likely to return to Japan after a few years' stay. Because recent newcomer families from Japan are from the most advantaged segments of society and are not permanent immigrants to the United States, they often have a special concern about the effect of their overseas stay on their children's education in the Japanese system.

The Japanese government tries to provide overseas education to as many of these students as possible. (These schools will be discussed in a subsequent chapter.) Further, now that 10,000 students per year return to Japan after living in various countries abroad, the Japanese Ministry of Education operates special assistance programs in designated schools all over Japan to help students readjust to the academic levels of the Japanese curriculum (*Status of Education of Children Overseas,* 1986, p. 67).

Japanese-American families, Japanese-born parents who live permanently in the United States, and Japanese families who are on short-term assignments in California may have overlapping but slightly varying interests in the strategies of the school program for their children. Each school and school district will need to plan such programs with the backgrounds and prospects of all these students in mind.

Location of Japanese Residents in the U.S.

Immigration records show that between 1861 and 1968 a total of 356,558 Japanese immigrated to the United States (Wilson and Hosokawa, 1982). The 1980 Census counted 261,817 persons of Japanese ethnicity in California, which is 37 percent of the total Japanese ethnic population in the United States (*Race of the Population by State,* 1980). Persons counted by the census as "Japanese" are Japanese Americans and Japanese nationals. The foreign Ministry of Japan reported a total of 146,104 Japanese citizens residing in the United States as of 1985 (*Statistics,* 1986).

In California the largest concentrations of both newcomer families from Japan and Japanese Americans live in the urban and suburban areas of Los Angeles, San Francisco, San Jose, Sacramento, Fresno, and San Diego. These concentrations are reflected in the number of Japanese-speaking students enrolled in California schools.

In the spring, 1985, California elementary and secondary schools counted a total of 10,129 students whose home language was Japanese. Of these, 3,679 students were limited-English proficient (LEP). The 36 school districts enrolling more than 20 LEP Japanese-speaking students were all in the greater Los Angeles, San Diego, or San Francisco Bay urban areas. Still, these top 36 districts enrolled less than three-fourths of the 3,697 LEP speakers of Japanese. The remaining 27 percent, or 1,010 students, attended another 222 school districts throughout the state. See Appendix A for the number of Japanese-speaking LEP students in each school district in 1986.

Japanese Residing in Other Countries

As of 1986, the island nation of Japan is home to about 120-million Japanese speakers. The largest population of Japanese speakers outside Japan is in Brazil, where the total Japanese and Japanese-Brazilian population is 750,000. Japanese immigration to Brazil began in 1908 and paralleled Japanese immigration to the United States. When Japanese immigrants were barred by the United States in the 1920s, immigration to Brazil was most vigorous (McDowell, 1980). Not all Japanese Brazilians today speak Japanese, as is the case among many of the 700,000 people in the United States of Japanese ethnicity.

According to the Japanese Foreign Ministry's count, there were 480,739 citizens of Japan living in foreign countries in 1985 (*Statistics,* 1986). Of that total, the largest numbers lived in the United States (146,104) and Brazil (120,276). Britain, Canada, and West Germany were the next-ranked countries, but they each hosted fewer than 20,000 Japanese citizens.

Occasionally, a school in California might find that a Korean adult or a native of Taiwan can speak Japanese fluently. Although exact figures are unavailable, persons raised in Korea or in Taiwan who attended Japanese-controlled schools prior to 1945 may be speakers of Japanese.

Quality of Education in Japan

The educational experience of children in Japan is a relatively homogeneous one in that the curriculum is standardized nationally, and education is compulsory for all children between six and fifteen years of age. As of 1980, school attendance by students of elementary and junior high school age was 99.98 percent. Of students of high school age, 93 percent were enrolled, and among university-aged youth, 33 percent attended institutions of higher education (*Education in Japan,* 1982, pp. 24–25). This rate of school attendance has risen dramatically over the last 100 years.

The development of universal education in Japan has gone hand-in-hand with the emergence of a highly technical society. Of the Meiji restoration, Edwin O. Reischauer (1974) observed that "one result . . . was to change Japanese society within a generation or two from one in which prestige and function were largely determined by birth to one in which both were determined almost entirely by education." The importance of education in this determination of one's prestige and function has led to a system that is intense and competitive, yet fosters a sense of group spirit and collective pride among schoolmates.

A postwar reorganization of the school system lent several "American" features to Japanese public education. Schooling is organized into six years of elementary school, three years of junior high school, three years of high school, and four years of university undergraduate study. The 1947 Fundamental Law of Education guarantees equal opportunity and prohibits discrimination on the basis of race, creed, sex, social or economic status, or family background. The curriculum emphasizes social studies, democratic political processes, and religious tolerance.

Yet, distinctions in individual ability begin to be drawn very early in the Japanese system, allowing only the most academically advanced students to gain entrance to the most prestigious college-preparatory junior and senior high schools. Public high schools as well as private ones require entrance examinations, and a recognized hierarchy among various options in public and private high schools emerges in each community. One's high school will have much to do with one's options for university education; therefore, both the last year of junior high school and the last year of high school, the entrance examination years, are pressure points in the educational career of college-bound students.

To master school subjects and ultimately to prepare themselves for the important entrance examinations, many students enroll in supplemental private schools called *juku*. A survey conducted by the Ministry of Education indicated that 47 percent of all ninth graders in Japan were attending a *juku* in 1986 (*Asahi Evening News,* April 9, 1986). These supplementary courses may be taught by a local neighborhood teacher in a home studio or may take the form of business franchises. Classes might be scheduled for every day after school or in special intensive sessions during school vacations. Because class size in public elementary and junior high schools is frequently over 40, *juku* allow for a degree of individualization by giving help in a particular subject or toward a particular goal of the student's choice. Some families in Japan forego *juku* in favor of a home tutor, *katei kyōshi*. The tutor, who often is a university student, usually meets twice weekly with the student in the home.

Fresh from this background, Japanese newcomers to California schools usually bring with them a good foundation in their basic subjects in Japanese. A high proportion of each student's time in the elementary years is spent in the development of reading, writing, and composition. The mathematical mastery of Japanese students usually surpasses the level of work expected at comparable grade levels in California. Social studies, science, music, art, and physical education are taught throughout the grade levels, and English is introduced from the first year of junior high school. Ronald S. Anderson (1975, p. 108) points out that the extended school calendar in Japan—sometimes 250 instructional days per year—can add up to an extra two full years of schooling compared to some American schools in the course of nine years of compulsory education. He proposes this as one reason Japanese students seem to be advanced in the skills areas.

Although some features of the Japanese school system correspond to the organization of American schools and many newcomer students are well prepared academically, California school personnel should become familiar with some of the differences between the two systems:

- In Japan kindergarten is not compulsory. Most preschools and kindergartens are operated privately and charge tuition. Children may attend kindergarten at age three, four, or five.
- Japanese children must be six years old before they enter first grade on April 1. This means that all children turn seven while in the first grade.
- The Japanese school year begins on April 1 and ends in March of the following year. Vacations are granted in summer, winter, and at the end of the school year in March.
- Elementary and junior high schools have three terms: early April to mid-July, late August to late December, and early January to late March. High schools are either on this three-term schedule or on a two-term schedule similar to the university calendar in Japan.
- School attendance and textbooks are free to all students in public schools in grades one through nine. In high schools, however, students must pay tuition fees and purchase their own textbooks at both public and private schools.
- A cafeteria lunch is provided at low cost to every elementary and junior high school student in Japan. It is usually against school rules to bring a lunch or food from home.
- Some form of school identification is worn by students from kindergarten through high school. Kindergarten students may wear matching hats and smocks over their play clothes. Elementary school students do not wear uniforms, but they must pin a plastic identification badge to their clothing every day. Junior and senior high school students usually wear school uniforms. Students are accustomed to a code of behavior while they are in their uniforms on their way to and from school. School rules also address appearance: no long hair among boys and no makeup or curled hair among the girls.

- Classes are self-contained at the elementary level; students do not break out for individualized instruction or other activities. The junior high school class stays together for all subjects, though teachers change. High school students also stay together as a class for most subjects.
- As in U.S. schools, elementary schools have grade levels from one through six. But the grades begin again at one in a Japanese junior high school and again in the first year of senior high school. The Japanese sixteen-year-old student who thinks he or she is in the "second grade" should be taught the American school's way of identifying the high school grade levels before a mistranslation results in an embarrassing situation.

Role of the Immigrant as Teacher or Tutor

A small proportion of adults from Japan are experienced teachers. Most Japanese who come to the U.S. for the purpose of teaching are university-level instructors. Elementary and secondary teachers from Japan are unlikely to come to California expecting to teach here, because of the differences of language and teacher certification in Japan and America. It is usually some circumstance other than a will to teach that brings an elementary or high school teacher to live in California. Some affirmative outreach on the part of California schools well may turn up experienced or potential teachers among speakers of Japanese in the community.

In Japan today most newly hired elementary and secondary teachers are graduates of universities, but this is a recent phenomenon. Half of all elementary school teachers and 30 percent of the junior high school teachers do not have a bachelor's degree. A few older teachers have a high school degree, and many have a junior college degree (*Education in Japan,* 1982, p. 77). However, all teachers have passed a rigorous examination in basic skills and pedagogy in order to get hired, so local Japanese school boards are assured of their teachers' competence. Thus, the school in California that is seeking a Japanese-speaking teacher must be careful about requiring a bachelor's degree, as this may discourage experienced teachers from stepping forward.

Two years in a junior college preparatory program for kindergarten teachers followed by some work experience in a nursery school is a common route to marriage for many Japanese women. Thus, wives and mothers in the Japanese-speaking community may be potential teachers of Japanese to young students. The term *teacher* may intimidate such women, and their own limitations in English may cause reluctance to work in the school setting; however, if the school can invite them into a particular, well-structured teaching or tutoring position, such women may prove to be a great resource.

Community college Japanese classes, adult school English classes, Japanese language schools run by the Japanese-speaking community, the foreign student office, and the Japanese language department of a local university are all likely places to locate potential Japanese-speaking teachers.

Attitudes of Japanese Parents

Japanese parents view education as the single most important key to their children's future success. In a highly industrialized and bureaucratized society where unskilled jobs are few, success in the competitive educational system is essential to a broad range of professions and vocations. Education is esteemed not only for its economic value in later life but also for the social status associated with a good education at the "right" schools.

Concerning the attitudes of Japanese parents, something of the difference between the role of the individual in Japanese society and in American society must be considered. It is the more typically American notion that each generation must do its own thing, that each individual must find a unique path to personal fulfillment, and that the emerging adult will be responsible only to himself or herself for the future of his or her own making. In contrast, within Japanese tradition each individual is the bearer of a family's continuity, and the reputation of the parents and the ancestors of each individual is reflected in his or her choices and deeds. Thus, it is incumbent on Japanese parents to take very good care to shape their children's sense of responsibility toward the family line and to provide every opportunity for the children's success in life to maintain the family line, the family business, and/or the family status. The fact that parents have been cared for in their old age within the house of one of their children—usually the eldest son—is only the outward expression of this sense that the emerging generation will always be responsible for maintaining their forebears, both in material and symbolic ways. This strong sense of mutual responsibility between the parents and their children has implications in educational attitudes.

Japanese families often make considerable sacrifices in order that their children can excel in their schoolwork and pass rigorous examinations for acceptance in the best junior high school, then in the best high school, and then in the best college. Reciprocally, children often sense that the entire hopes of the family are pinned on their own academic performance, and the children are anxious about fulfilling parental expectations. When groups of high school students in Japan and the United States were asked, "Are your parents proud of you?" only 4.9 percent of the American students replied

"No," whereas 50.8 percent of the Japanese students answered "No" (*Facts and Figures of Japan,* 1980).

Further surveys reveal the centrality of education in family values: asked to rank desirable attributes of a spouse, both husbands and wives declared it highly important that their spouse be zealous about their children's education (Cummings, 1980). Housewives frequently revealed that their main concern in childrearing is to facilitate their children's success in the schools (Sumiya, 1967). Japanese mothers smilingly apply a special expression to themselves as individuals or as a group concerned with pushing their children's academic success: *kyōiku mama* or, literally, "education mama."

A corollary to the high regard held by the Japanese for education is a correspondingly high regard for educators. Teachers are esteemed as role models for the community; they are expected to be correct and compassionate in their behavior at all times. Teachers in Japan are by and large quite conscious of this status and strive to lead exemplary lives in their communities. In direct terms this means that each teacher frequently calls on students' families and provides many counseling and guidance functions among the families and youngsters. In indirect terms this means that the teacher consciously adopts very conservative social behavior in the community—refraining from visiting coffee shops, from playing *pachinko* in the amusement halls, even from wearing bright colors, or from any other behavior of marginal propriety in traditional Japanese culture.

Japanese parents are accustomed to maintaining close contact with their child's teacher and others who are influential in the child's education. The Congress of Parents and Teachers, Inc., has become a familiar organization nationwide in Japan, and it is generally active at each school site. Parents play a supportive role at the school and are highly respectful of the teachers and school authorities. In Japan parents usually defer to the judgment of the teacher about school matters and hesitate to express opinions that are independent of or different from the teacher's opinion or the school policy.

In Japanese schools there are no teachers' aides or parent volunteers in the classroom; parents participate only in extracurricular activities such as study trips and school festivals. The staff in California schools should orient the parents of newcomer students to parent involvement opportunities and invite them to participate in activities that match their capabilities. The mothers in families on temporary assignment from Japan might welcome the chance to get involved in the public school as a chance to socialize outside the home.

Chapter II

Historical and Sociocultural Factors Concerning the Japanese Language

The topics discussed in this chapter are Japanese language education and language use in social settings both in Japan and in California. In years past it might have been said that the place of the Japanese language was either in Japan or in the minority Japanese-American community in the United States. Increasingly, however, Japanese-English binguality is an essential and integral feature of business, finance, law, tourism, citizens' movements, government, and the arts both in Japan and in California. Japanese language courses in the universities are overflowing with students in the 1980s, partly because job prospects for bilingual individuals in any field are very good. Although it has not always been the case, both Japanese and English language education are now universally offered to young people in Japan, and Japanese language education for all levels of students is thriving in public schools and weekend schools throughout California today.

Language Education in Japan

The Statistics Bureau of the Japanese government reports that 99.7 percent of all Japanese over fifteen years of age are literate (*Facts and Figures of Japan,* 1980). Although "literate" is not clearly defined by this source, the national educational curriculum introduces the most commonly used characters in the written Japanese language, such as those required to read most newspapers, by grade six. By the time students reach grade nine, their reading vocabulary and reference skills are thoroughly developed to meet everyday demands. With 99.9 percent of the population completing nine years of schooling today (*Facts About Japan,* 1979), Japan has achieved a highly and uniformly literate population.

Attitudes Toward Reading and Writing Skills

Historically, the written form of the Japanese language was developed in the sixth and seventh centuries, when, from contacts with Chinese civilization, the Japanese adopted the idea of writing down their oral language. Not only were many Chinese characters adopted to represent Japanese words, but also the attitudes toward

15

literacy seem to have been adopted from the Buddhist and Confucian traditions as well: great value is placed on reading and writing skills and knowledge of the literary classics, and the literate individual is highly respected.

During the middle ages in Japan, as in the West, priestly orders (Buddhist rather than Christian priestly orders in Japan, of course) served to transmit literacy skills to young men. Even until the establishment of public education in the late 1800s, "temple schools" were the centers of education in each community. Perhaps this tradition perpetuated the high esteem for the written word, the sanctity of study, and the righteousness of the scholar. Today, good reading and writing skills are not only essential from a pragmatic point of view, but still are valued highly out of a deep respect for scholastic excellence and the aesthetic beauty of the written language.

While English speakers can fairly easily type their language, typewriting in Japanese is a specialized and time-consuming skill, requiring a much more complicated typewriter. Thus, in schools and businesses, many functions that Americans find in typewritten form are still handwritten in Japan. For this reason clear and neat handwriting is a skill that is emphasized in Japan. It interests Americans that a fountain pen is regarded in Japan as the most proper means of writing a letter, a resume, or other important document. A felt-tip pen or a ballpoint pen may be fine for informal uses, but they do not represent a person well for serious purposes!

Even moving beyond the practical level of interest in good handwriting, the Japanese love the written script itself. Brush and ink calligraphy is a fine art. Written quotations from poetry decorate scrolls, paintings, and ceramics as much for the artistry of the written characters as for the meaning that the characters convey.

Learning to Read and Write Japanese

Formal reading instruction begins in the first grade in Japan, but even before entering school, children learn to recognize some written words in their everyday environment. All three kinds of symbols used in Japanese writing usually can be recognized by the preschool child: the Chinese-derived *kanji* logographs that say *Entry* or *Exit* on doors, for example; the cursive phonetic *hiragana* syllabary that is used in storybooks for very young children, for example; and the other phonetic syllabary, called *katakana,* often used to transliterate foreign words, such as *bus,* into Japanese. Children usually learn to write their own name in either *kanji* or *hiragana* before going to school. Students who attend kindergarten learn to recognize more words through games, felt-board stories, or flash-card drills. Thus, researchers seeking nonreading Japanese children for a study of reading acquisition had to limit their subjects to three- and four-year-old children, because the five- and six-year-olds were already too familiar with many written words (Steinberg and Yamada, 1978-79).

Students enter the first grade after they pass their sixth birthday; at that time instruction in reading and writing begins in earnest. The subject of reading and writing Japanese is called *kokugo* or "national language." *Kokugo* remains a required subject in every grade level through the nine years of compulsory education. In the early elementary school years, instruction in reading and writing consumes almost one-third of the total required instructional hours (*Education in Japan,* 1982, p. 59). Instructional objectives and a sequence of written characters are prescribed for each grade level by the Ministry of Education.

The phonetic *hiragana* syllabary is taught in the first grade as the first system by which children read and write sentences. The second phonetic syllabary, *katakana,* is introduced in the first grade as well, but the official national curriculum does not expect students to be able to write *katakana* until the second grade. *Kanji,* the logographs derived from Chinese, are introduced in each grade level in a prescribed sequence. First graders learn about 70 characters, second graders should know a total of 220, third graders should know a total of 410, and so on. By the end of the sixth grade, students should be able to recognize and write about 1,000 characters (*Course of Study for Elementary Schools in Japan,* 1983). (See also Appendix C.)

Junior high school students in Japan continue to learn to recognize an additional 700 or so *kanji* and practice writing new compound words using all the characters they have learned since elementary school. In high school the national curriculum mandates only one year of *kokugo* for all students, but most students in academic high schools continue reading Japanese literature through the eleventh and twelfth grades as well.

Reading for Enjoyment

A rich supply of varied and inexpensive reading material is aimed at the young reading population in Japan. Every neighborhood has its newsstand or bookstore offering educational and recreational reading materials for all ages and all interests. With a tendency to identify with a particular hobby even from a young age, students become avid readers of nonfiction subjects such as sports, nature, history, crafts, and music. Many students purchase thin paperback accompaniments to daily or weekly educational media broadcasts relating to their school subjects and hobbies. Magazines and serialized comic books geared to children or teenagers provide further recreational reading.

Using Writing Skills

In the school setting students use their writing skills by answering assigned questions relating to their reading or by researching and reporting on social or scientific questions. In addition, they practice *sakubun,* which is "creative composition."

The art of calligraphy with a bamboo brush and black ink is introduced, to a limited extent, in schools beginning in the third grade. Some students continue to practice brush-writing as a hobby with a local *shuji* master. This writing skill is practiced as an art form, together with many of the overtones of self-discipline and meditation associated with other traditional Japanese arts, rather than for the practical necessity of brush-writing. The students' best work is displayed at school fairs or at community festivals. Families bring out the brush and inkstone on January 1 of each year to write greeting cards and to write auspicious calligraphy and poetry to welcome in the New Year. Certain formal occasions, such as signing a guest book at a wedding, require a good hand with a bamboo brush, so students and adults are conscious that they need a minimal level of skill and practice to cope gracefully.

The conventions of letter-writing are taught in school, and some students become active letter writers in their free time. Some have pen pals or friends in other regions of Japan to correspond with in Japanese. When students begin to learn foreign languages, some adopt pen pals outside Japan, as well.

Attitudes Toward Oral Skills

The Japanese appreciate well-developed oral skills in a young person just as Americans do, but the definitions of just what those skills are might be quite different in the views of Japanese and Americans. These differences are at the heart of the distinction in the relationships of individuals, particularly young individuals, to elders or to the group at large, as experienced and expected in Japan and the United States. Although any attempt to characterize these differences runs the risk of cultural stereotyping, a few exaggerated examples of traditional differences in values are listed on the following page. Any individual in either culture may fall anywhere on the spectrum of personal style. But it might be helpful for the American educator to remember that in a new school setting, the anxious Japanese youth may resort to some of the most traditional and polite conversational behaviors according to Japanese standards. Teachers can help explain the different behaviors or conventions of the two cultures. A few such conventions are illustrated as follows:

Conventions and values in oral Japanese in Japan	*Conventions and values in oral English in U.S.*
A Japanese youth . . .	An American youth . . .
Should bow to show respect, but should not initiate a conversation with an elder.	Should smile and make friendly conversation on greeting an elder.
Must choose differentiated vocabulary and verb forms to speak politely to a "superior." Knows that the wrong use of expressions may constitute an affront to the superior status of the listener.	Does not differentiate word choices as radically when speaking to a teacher or a parent's friend. Does not even perceive these adults to be "superior." Will "be oneself" in all situations.
Will never use the name of an adult when speaking face-to-face. Will call the instructor or the priest *sensei,* meaning "teacher," rather than by name.	Politely calls adults "Mrs. Jones" or "Mr. Smith." It is rude to address an instructor merely as "teacher."
Will not insult the teacher's efforts by saying, "I don't understand." Will nod politely even while not understanding and attribute the difficulty to his or her own lack of diligence.	Should speak up whenever he or she does not understand. This is a favor to the teacher and the other students as well. Perceives his or her own learning to depend on good or bad teaching.
Should remain silent rather than exhibiting faulty understanding or command of a skill. To put forth a mistaken answer or an unperfected skill is a personal disgrace and an insult to the teacher and the discipline.	Will give his or her best effort to answer a question or do a particular task, because trying is more important than being absolutely correct. Though just a beginner, he or she will not hesitate to demonstrate or speak about a particular field.
Will hesitate to express his or her own opinion, for fear that it may sound presumptuous or run contrary to the feelings of the teacher.	Should be able to give his or her own view on a topic when called on by the teacher and to defend his or her statements with reasonable arguments.
Must always defer to the judgment of superiors and must never openly disagree with anyone. To be contentious is a sign of conceit.	Is encouraged to develop an independent viewpoint and to express it in contrast to the view of the teacher or other students. Debating is a high-level oral skill.

Developing Oral Language

Educators in Japanese schools do not overtly concern themselves with "oral language development" in the curriculum. The school does, however, serve an important function in shaping the oral language habits of the students. Customary American forms of oral language practice are not found in the Japanese school; for example, there is no "show and tell" in the early grades and no speech or forensic classes in the upper grades. As a vehicle of the traditional culture in Japan, the school does not emphasize spontaneity of speech or individuality of expression in front of the group.

Rather, one important function of the school is to assist the child to become aware of the differences in levels of formality of the oral language that are used by children in the home and which they may continue to use at home and that used by mature persons in conversing with other adults outside the family setting. Students' mastery of these differences during their school years will be one of the most important preparations for well-adjusted adult life. Included in this schooling process is the distinction of standard dialectical patterns of speech from regional forms of speech. Just as educators in American schools convey an implicit preference for "standard" English, educators in Japanese schools model and encourage the use of "standard" and "polite" Japanese.

Educators in Japanese schools achieve this by a literary and model-oriented approach. In school, as well as at home, stories are read to children in which various characters exhibit speech appropriate to their social relations with each other. Even from the earliest reading and writing exercises, the modeling of forms of polite oral language is one of the implicit functions of paper-and-pencil work. Teachers model very polite speech and will sometimes prompt students to use polite forms of speech to them or to other adults in the school. The student who persists in speaking out in speech forms that are familiar rather than polite becomes the class "discipline problem." Forms of speech that are quite acceptable from preschool children begin to sound like gruff gangland talk when used by adolescents, so schools and parents place great emphasis on the mastery of polite oral Japanese during the school years. The implications for the student whose native language is Japanese but who never receives formal training in the Japanese language are obvious here. The childlike level of language will not pass for acceptable Japanese in adulthood.

Developing Attitudes About Speaking

Reticence is valued in the presence of elders and superiors in Japanese culture, and the school complements the home in imbuing this value in youngsters. Furthermore, even when it is one's prerogative to speak, simple and brief remarks are valued over lengthy or pointed statements. Brevity is considered to show humility and respect for the intuitions of the listeners (Ueda, 1974). The person who is glib is not particularly respected in Japan; rather, he or she is to be somewhat mistrusted. Traditional fairy tales concerning "The Monkey and the Crab" show the smooth-talking crab to be quite a disreputable character. Japanese will point out that their nation has never produced a great orator or even a notable historical speech.

Students from Japan who are accustomed to fewer demands for oral responses within formal school lessons may not be accustomed to volunteering verbal responses or to oral reporting as expected in the American classroom.

The answers to the following questions that were asked of groups of Japanese and American college students in their respective countries reveal differences in preferences that have been conditioned by the two schooling systems (Hachiya, 1974):

How would you respond in class to a question to which you knew the answer?
61 percent of the Japanese students said, "Prefer not to answer at all."
34 percent of the American students said, "Prefer not to answer at all."

Given a choice between turning in a paper and delivering an oral report, which would you choose?
21 percent of the Japanese students said, "Give the oral report."
41 percent of the American students said, "Give the oral report."

Learning English in Japan

English becomes a compulsory subject for almost all students in Japan in the first year of junior high school and continues to be required in each year until high school graduation. During these six years, students move from the introduction of the Roman alphabet to the reading of classical excerpts from Dickens and Shakespeare. The emphasis in English teaching has focused on reading and the ability to translate written English passages into Japanese. Until recent years, Japanese teachers of English have been confined in their training and experience to the study of literary English, and speaking and conversation have not figured actively in the teaching of English as a foreign language in secondary schools. Increasingly, however, as students and teachers have enjoyed more practice of their spoken English through coming in contact with English that is used in the media or by visiting English-speaking countries, activities in English language classes offer more opportunities to learn conversational skills in this foreign language.

The goals of English education in Japan follow the ideals of the educational modernization undertaken with the Meiji Restoration in 1868, when Japan looked to the languages as well as to the technology of the West to assume a world role alongside other industrialized nations. In some high schools and in many universities, students study another foreign language in addition to English—Chinese, French, German, Russian, or Spanish are the most common choices. In the nineteenth and early twentieth centuries, the English of England was the standard English taught in Japan, although in the last 30 years the standard has become oriented more toward American spelling, idioms, and pronunciation.

When asked, "Why are you studying English?" many Japanese high school students will smilingly reply, "To get into college." English has become one of the competitive subject areas that serve as a rigorous sorting mechanism to allow only a select stratum of young scholars to enter Japan's top universities and colleges each year.

Using English in Japan

English is used in Japan by persons engaged in diplomacy, international trade, and tourism in the larger urban centers, where communication with English speakers from other parts of the globe is essential. Several English-language daily newspapers are published in Japan's largest cities, mainly for non-Japanese-speaking readers. Tokyo now has one English-medium television station, and several English-language programs are broadcast regularly on the Japanese-language radio and television stations. A new "simulcast" feature built in to Japanese television sets allows viewers to tune in to either the English soundtrack or the Japanese soundtrack of movies and TV programs originally produced in English-speaking countries. Movie theaters throughout Japan run English-language films from England and the United States, with the added benefit of Japanese subtitles (or sidetitles, running vertically along the side of the screen) for most of the viewing public.

Japanese students and adults who are learning English may follow daily English language lessons on educational radio or television. Paperback workbooks that accompany these lessons are available at many local newsstands. Through such ready access to English media and instruction, many Japanese have a passive familiarity with English, even though they are not fluent speakers of English.

On the level of "loan words," English is quite frequently used in the vocabulary of every Japanese. Along with the adoption of certain realms of technology from the West, the labels, usually English, for these concepts or objects have been adopted into Japanese as well. The following are a few examples of the way in which an English word becomes transformed into a Japanese word with a more or less obvious phonetic relation to the English original:

English	Japanese
shower	*shawa*
radio	*rajio*
cancel	*kyanseru*
mass communications	*masukomi*

Even though English loan words have infused the technical vocabularies of many scientific fields of study, all subjects at the university level are taught entirely in Japanese; even advanced scientific research and reporting are conducted in Japanese.

Language Education in California

Japanese who immigrated to California before the Exclusion Act of 1924 and their children born between the 1880s and the 1940s experienced a very different situation than did those Japanese who immigrated or came to work in the United States after the liberalization of immigration in the 1950s. The prewar and wartime experiences of Japanese Americans had particular repercussions on the use of language in the community. Recent newcomers from Japan are in a very different personal situation and social milieu, but preservation and loss of language are still matters of concern.

From 1900 to the eve of World War II, certain California business, labor, and publishing interests raised loud charges of encroaching Japanese colonialism and unfair economic competition by Japanese immigrants and their families on the West Coast. This clamor pressured many Japanese into segregated schools and "Japan Town" communities and pressured some *issei* and *nisei* to repudiate outwardly their Japanese language and cultural heritage. Privately, however, many Japanese moved to establish language schools to maintain their language and culture. The humiliation of anyone speaking Japanese in America at the outbreak of America's involvement in World War II, violent acts against American citizens of Japanese descent, and the mass internment of 110,000 Japanese-American *issei* and *nisei* during the war years were further shocks, leaving individuals little choice but to make an active display of loyalty to the United States and to conform to ways considered stereotypically "American." Although personal memories and interpretations of these experiences vary, certain general effects are still felt in the Japanese-American community (*The Experience of Japanese Americans in the United States,* 1974). Concerning language use, these pressures undoubtedly hastened the loss of the Japanese language among *nisei* and succeeding generations. Concerning school, these pressures reinforced an attitude of determination toward educational gains and personal achievement. Among some third- and fourth-generation Japanese Americans, the historical injustices suffered by their parents and grandparents have stimulated a renewed interest in their Japanese heritage and a heightened sense of personal and cultural rights, sometimes manifested in a desire to restore Japanese language abilities in their own families.

This history must be borne in mind whenever Japanese Americans are singled out as a group that demonstrates that bilingual education is not necessary or as a model of "assimilation" into the English language and American life-style. Many aspects of Japanese heritage were suppressed among Japanese Americans between 1900 and 1945 at great cost—of property, of dignity, of opportunities.

Japanese immigrating to California during the last 30 years do not share the experiences mentioned above. Recent newcomers from Japan may not know very much about Japanese Americans. Ties between the community of *shōsha* business families here on temporary assignment and the permanent Japanese-American community vary today, depending on personal acquaintances and organizational affiliations. Individual Japanese nationals and Japanese Americans hold some sociocultural traditions and values in common, but they may also maintain distinct expectations about their children's language and schooling in California.

Even though Japanese newcomer families face a relatively positive social atmosphere as compared to the history of earlier generations of immigrants, language loss is still a concern to many families. In one study of 48 Japanese sixth-grade children temporarily residing in the United States, even though all the students attended a weekend Japanese school and 80 percent of their parents strongly hoped for the maintenance of high Japanese skills, 21 of the students were evaluated as low in Japanese skills (Okamoto-Bichard, 1985). Although overt or large-scale social suppression is not a factor for these children, language loss continues among some.

Use of English Outside School

Rarely in California are Japanese-speaking families so geographically concentrated as to be unexposed to or isolated from the English-speaking "mainstream." In community businesses or activities that are ethnically Japanese, English will often be actively used by some while Japanese is spoken by others. Children from Japanese-speaking families are accustomed to hearing English outside their homes in stores and businesses and on the street. Some are exposed to English at church or youth group meetings. Most of these children also have contact with English through neighborhood children and by watching television or listening to the radio even before they attend kindergarten. Some small children, however, who remain close to their Japanese-speaking mothers may be quite limited in their contact with English—especially in direct interaction with English speakers—until they begin school.

Use of Japanese Language Skills

Japanese bilingual communities develop their children's Japanese language skills in a variety of ways. Most of these communities provide instruction in Japanese schools. These schools operate on a variety of schedules and have a number of affiliations. They generally can be divided into two types. One type of school is primarily for American-born Japanese and concentrates on the Japanese language and culture. The other type is for Japanese nationals who are temporarily residing in the United States. These schools include regular academic subjects and are designed to help students maintain their school achievement with their peers in Japan. It is important to note, however, that many Japanese Americans send their children to this latter type of school for more intensive Japanese language development. They may also extend the former type of school beyond the usual Saturday-only schedule to weekday evenings or afternoons to further their children's study of Japanese. A list of these schools is presented in Appendix B.

The first type of school serves to teach the elements of Japanese conversation, reading, and writing to children who are by and large American born and who are usually more fluent and literate in English than in Japanese. In the community such schools are known as *Nihongo Gakkō,* literally "Japanese language schools." By supporting these schools, the community and individual parents demonstrate that they value bilingualism and an understanding of Japanese cultural heritage among their children. These schools usually are sponsored by the local Japanese-American community affiliated with a particular Buddhist or Christian church or by an independent organization of parents who request respected educators within the Japanese bilingual community to conduct Saturday classes for their youngsters. These classes and schools are supported by monthly student fees and special fund-raising activities. While Japanese language schools for Japanese-American students often provide a thorough and sequential opportunity for students to learn the Japanese language and aspects of Japanese culture, the offerings of this first type of school are not related directly to the curriculum of the public schools in Japan.

A second type of school serves students who are fluent in Japanese and who wish to keep up with the academic curriculum of the

Japanese school system. This type of school is known in the community as the *Nihonjin Gakkō,* or "Japanese people's school," although sometimes it also is referred to as *Nihongo Gakkō.* While a few of the students at these schools are American-born students whose Japanese has become "good enough" at home or at Japanese language school, most of the students at the *Nihonjin Gakkō* recently have come from Japan and will probably return to Japan. The children of most Japanese businesspersons who come to reside temporarily in the metropolitan areas of California attend the *Nihonjin Gakkō* on Saturdays to keep up with their Japanese studies. The instructional day is a long and intensive one. Students in grade levels one through eleven study the material that has been introduced in the nationally standardized curricula of every Japanese school in four areas: Japanese, mathematics, science, and social studies.

On a visit to a *Nihonjin Gakkō,* two of the authors of this handbook asked if students did not mind spending their Saturdays in school. Teachers and students both responded that, since Saturday is a school day in Japan and since the students whose English is limited feel particularly anxious in their American schools, attending this Japanese school every Saturday seemed natural and even enjoyable.

In California, students and faculty travel for many miles to attend the *Nihonjin Gakkō,* which is held in schools rented from the public school system. One junior high school in San Francisco is filled with 630 Japanese-speaking students attending *Nihonjin Gakkō* every Saturday, while in Los Angeles about 2,000 Japanese-speaking students are enrolled in four schools. The teachers of the Japanese schools usually are bilingual professionals, including some public school teachers and university professors who completed their education in Japan but now are settled permanently in California. The principals of the San Francisco and Los Angeles schools, like their counterparts in many other cities outside Japan, are outstanding Japanese educational leaders chosen for a three-year assignment as the administrators of Japanese overseas schools. These schools receive administrative guidance in addition to curricular and financial support from the Ministry of Education in Japan (though students also pay nominal fees to attend). The instructional materials include the currently authorized textbooks and teaching guides that are used throughout Japan. The school year calendar of these schools follows the April-to-March school year of Japan to ensure some degree of continuity for the student who has just arrived from Japan or who leaves California to reenroll in school in Japan.

Many local school districts in California have established a system of formal recognition on students' transcripts of studies completed in both kinds of Japanese schools conducted on Saturdays. Credit is granted for Japanese as a foreign language or for academic subjects, such as geometry or world history, undertaken in the Japanese language. Public school districts in California whose Japanese-speaking students are able to attend a well-established Japanese school usually find this community resource a valuable complement to the program within the public school. Particularly for the limited-English-proficient student, the public school personnel can do well to articulate with the program objectives of the private "Japanese language school" or "Japanese people's school."

Use of the Japanese Language in the Community

Many organizations and traditional events provide settings in which speakers of Japanese naturally speak Japanese. These events are supported or sponsored by community groups, Japanese businesses and corporations, churches, or the Japanese government. Such settings include Japanese language schools, cultural events, fund-raisers, community education activities, and so forth.

In addition, daily family and community activities provide individuals who are dominant in Japanese opportunities to use their language to carry out normal functions related to their lives in the United States. The Japanese language can be heard in restaurants, movie houses, travel agencies, bookstores, and gift shops. It is also part of the daily life of many Japanese people who use Japanese when they are with members of their own families. Such language use has many consequences beyond allowing people to communicate naturally; for example, when they use Japanese, these individuals are developing a language of international importance and, at the same time, they are reinforcing their cultural identity.

Japanese-language churches provide fellowship and social support for speakers of Japanese. Newcomers from Japan who are Christian might attend a Japanese bilingual church. If not Christian, a newcomer family may be invited to a Buddhist church, which is actually an "American" phenomenon, new to most Japanese. (Buddhism in Japan is more individualistic than congregational and more functional only in funerary services than in the activities of Sunday worship, Sunday school, or weddings, which are conducted by Buddhist churches in America.)

Associations of persons from the same region of Japan, called *kenjinkai,* are active in some California cities, as are organizations specifically serving senior Japanese Americans or newcomer families. Japanese is spoken in the activities of such organizations.

While English also might be used comfortably by bilingual persons in the activities mentioned above, English is least likely to take over the vocabularies or events that are specific to the Japanese culture.

When no English counterpart exists for a Japanese event, ritual, or food, the Japanese phrases or words stay in circulation even among young Japanese Americans who know little Japanese. Thus, the language used during the holidays, at memorial services, or in describing feelings that are particularly "Japanese" probably will remain Japanese.

Chapter III
Linguistic Characteristics of the Japanese Language

Many speakers of English find the Japanese language intriguing for its structural differences from Indo-European languages, for its characteristic writing system, and for the special ways in which cultural features are embedded in language habits. This chapter includes a brief history of the Japanese language, a discussion of the differences between the Japanese and English languages, and a description of the ways in which cultural patterns are reflected in the Japanese language.

Although this chapter takes a contrastive approach primarily for the information of school staff who do not know the Japanese language, two cautions should be expressed. First, Japanese and English are overwhelmingly similar in their functions in the societies that use them: all human feelings and transactions are possible and are practiced in both languages all the time. Fundamental differences in personality or outlook on the basis of language alone do not appear to exist. Persons on either side of the language "barrier" have a great deal in common, even though a comparison of their two languages may indicate numerous differences. Second, for the sake of clarification and expansion and concrete understanding, the summaries of the features of the Japanese language in this section are intended for bilingual personnel and school staff who do not know Japanese. Better yet, for attaining a sense of the nature of the Japanese language, there is no substitute for studying Japanese.

Origin of the Japanese Language

The questions of the origin of the Japanese language and its kinship with other modern languages have interested linguists for over a century, and lively debate continues in the academic literature to this day. A few points are indisputable. The Japanese language is not linguistically related to Chinese, despite the similar appearance of the two writing systems to Western eyes. The Japanese borrowed written Chinese characters, many vocabulary words, and many cultural concepts, but Japanese was a completely distinct language even at the time of these borrowings—about the sixth century, A.D. As a tone language in which most words are only one syllable, the Chinese

29

language belongs to the Sino-Tibetan family of languages. Japanese words, in contrast, are usually two or more syllables in length, strung together in an agglutinative fashion, with many small units of meaning linked together as in a chain. Structurally, Japanese is clearly not akin to Chinese in its origins. With equal certainty, Japanese is known to be closely related to the Okinawan language.

Scholars have posited relationships between Japanese and many other languages of Asia and the Pacific: Formosan, Indonesian, Melanesian, Polynesian, Malayan, Mon-Khmer, and Tibeto-Burman languages. Most of these theories spring from limited lists of "sound-alike" words having similar meanings in the two languages being compared. Today, most of these correspondences are dismissed as either chance, borrowing, or at best, as an historical infusion into a particular early strata of the Japanese language (Ono, 1970).

The most successful and widely accepted explanation of the origin of the Japanese language—although one still in the process of debate and reformulation—relates it to the Altaic language family, which includes Turkish, Mongol, Manchu, and Korean. This hypothesis began with enthusiastic listings of "sound-alike" words in Japanese and Korean as well as observations of similarity in syntactic patterns by Japanese and Western scholars about the turn of the century (Kanazawa, 1910). Did these correlations establish genetic relationships between the two languages, or did they merely indicate heavy borrowing during intense cultural contact with Korea around the dawn of Japanese history? This question has engendered much further scholarship in pursuit of regular phonological correspondences that can relate old Japanese and Korean to a common ancestral language. The reconstruction of a proto-Altaic language and the discovery of an early "linguistic unity" covering the Korean Peninsula and the Japanese Archipelago is now the aim of historians of both the Japanese and Korean languages (Miller, 1971).

Dialectical Differences

The linguistic diversity that characterizes many island nations of Asia—such as Indonesia or the Philippines—is not nearly so pronounced in Japan. Japan's regional dialects were more prevalent in the last century, but the spread of compulsory education and radio and television has reduced dialectical differences to insignificance among the younger generation. Although many students are familiar with local dialects, they have learned standard Japanese in school.

Okinawan is closely related to Japanese but is quite different; sometimes it is considered a dialect and sometimes a separate language. Okinawan students learn standard Japanese at school, but the use of Okinawan remains very strong in the home and community.

Only in the case of Okinawan parents or children might there be a problem of communication with the speakers of Japanese in California schools.

Differences Between Japanese and English

It is not surprising that the Japanese language—having been derived from origins far removed from Indo-European languages—should not lend itself to simple or easy description by the terminology or methodology of the grammarians of Western languages. Nevertheless, it is possible to list some of the basic differences between Japanese and English. Because library resources on the Japanese language are extensive, the discussion here will emphasize only the basic distinctions that the Japanese speaker will face when learning English.

Although "contrastive" familiarity with these differences may be helpful to the school staff, the differences should not be the primary bases for lesson plans. Nor will the differences between the two languages necessarily predict the errors that students will make when learning the second language. Current pedagogical research minimizes the significance of the specific features of the first language in acquiring a second language and indicates that a grammar-based approach to the teaching of a second language should be rejected in favor of an emphasis on communicative competence. Theories concerning the ways in which two languages interact in the mental process an individual goes through in becoming bilingual and practical methods for teaching a second language are described in this document's companion volume, *Schooling and Language Minority Students: A Theoretical Framework* (1981).

Japanese grammar. Japanese and English words are classified as nouns, verbs, and adjectives, but words in these categories behave differently in the two languages, as indicated in the following examples:

1. Japanese nouns are the same in singular and plural. There is no such marker as the "-s" ending in English to denote a plural in Japanese. Only the context will reveal if a noun is singular or plural.
2. Japanese nouns are not preceded by an article such as *the* or *a* in English.
3. Because there is no singular-plural distinction in Japanese, there is no corresponding distinction between *this* (singular pronoun) and *these* (plural pronoun) or between *that* and *those*. *This* and *that* functions are performed by particular words in Japanese, but without distinction according to the number of the pronoun.

31

4. In Japanese there is no parallel for the distinctions made in English between modifiers of nouns that are "countable," such as marbles, days, or flavors, and modifiers of nouns that are "uncountable," such as sugar, advice, or money. Modifiers that indicate quantity, such as *much, many, a few,* and *a little,* are applied to countable and uncountable nouns differently in English; for example, it is wrong to say "much shoes" or "many patience."

5. Pronouns rarely are used in Japanese speech, as compared to English, and even more rarely used in writing. In fact, linguists usually say the Japanese language has no pronouns, as such. Although several Japanese "demonstratives" may be used to say *I* or *you* or *he,* these words are avoided as much as possible in polite communication. A Japanese speaker usually chooses a related noun or verb to express all the functions of English pronouns (I, me, mine, my, you, yours, your, he, him, his, she, her, hers, it, its, we, us, our, ours, they, their, theirs, them).

6. For the purpose of verb tense, Japanese time is divided into past and nonpast, while English time is divided into past, present, and future. Only the context in Japanese distinguishes whether a verb is happening at present or will happen in the future. There is no parallel in Japanese for the perfect tenses in English. The present perfect tense, for example, "I have eaten," may only be expressed by the simple past tense in Japanese.

7. The Japanese language has no modal or auxiliary verb forms such as, for example, "might eat" or "should have eaten." But the stems of ten possible endings for each Japanese verb perform many variations on the sense of the verb:

English verb "eat"	Japanese verb *tabe* + ending
let's eat	*tabeyo*
probably ate	*tabetaro*
provided that (one) eats	*tabereba*

8. The Japanese adjective, like the verb, is highly inflected; for example, there are nine different endings on the stem of an adjective qualifying the sense of the adjective. Separate words are used in English to qualify the adjective:

English adjective "long"	Japanese adjective *naga* + ending
is long (present tense)	*nagai*
was long (past tense)	*nagakatta*
if it is long (conditional)	*nagakattara*

Japanese syntax. The way in which words are put together into sentences or phrases in Japanese is quite different from English usage. The main variables in Japanese are (1) its use of "particles" to mark

32

syntactical functions of words; (2) its word order; and (3) the distinctive process of agglutination.

1. "Particles" are units of the Japanese language, usually brief sounds inserted after the main elements of a sentence. For example, *wa* or *ga* marks the word or phrase that is the subject of the sentence; *o* marks that word or phrase that is the direct object of the verb. The function of English prepositions is also served by particles following a noun in Japanese.

English	Japanese
to Tokyo	*Tokyo e*
from Tokyo	*Tokyo kara*
in Tokyo	*Tokyo de*

No Japanese sentence is complete without the proper use of particles, as in this example:

sensei	*wa*	*tegami*	*o*
teacher	subject particle	letter	object particle

Tokyo	*kara*	*dashimashita*
Tokyo	from	sent

English translation: "The teacher sent the letter from Tokyo."

The particle *ka* or *yo* added to the end of the preceding Japanese sentence would make the sentence a question or an emphatic statement. The particle *ka* can function as a question mark in English:

sensei	*wa*	*tegami*	*o*
teacher	subject particle	letter	object particle

Tokyo	*kara*	*dashimashita*	*ka*
Tokyo	from	sent	question particle

English translation: "Did the teacher send the letter from Tokyo?"

Likewise, the particle *yo* can function as an exclamation point in English to add emphasis or register surprise:

sensei	*wa*	*tegami*	*o*
teacher	subject particle	letter	object particle

Tokyo	*kara*	*dashimashita*	*yo*
Tokyo	from	sent	exclamation particle

English translation: "The teacher sent the letter from Tokyo!"

2. Word order differs between Japanese and English. The usual word order in English is: subject verb object, as in: "Mary loves John." If we switch the position of subject and object, this sentence totally changes its meaning to "John loves Mary." Word order itself lends meaning in English. In Japanese, however, word order is quite flexible, as long as the particle marking a word's function in the sentence stays attached to the word. The usual word order in Japanese is: subject object verb, as in:

Mary	*wa*	*John*	*o*	*aishiteimasu*
Mary	subject marker	John	object marker	loves

But this sentence means the same thing:

John	*o*	*Mary*	*wa*	*aishiteimasu*
John	object marker	Mary	subject marker	loves

Another difference in the order of elements in Japanese and English sentences is whether or not there is even an explicit subject. An explicit subject element is not structurally required in a Japanese sentence, especially when the subject would be expressed in English by a pronoun.

Nihon	*kara*	*irrashaimashita*	*ka*
Japan	from	came (hono-rific)	question particle

English translation: "Did you come from Japan?"

(This *you* is implied by the honorific verb.)

A third major distinction in word order concerns the placement of subordinate clauses. In English a subordinate clause most often follows the word that it modifies, as in:

The cookies **that John ate.**

In Japanese the clause *that John ate* precedes the word it modifies, as in:

John	*no*	*tabeta*	*kukki*
John	agent particle	ate	cookies

Likewise,

John ate the cookies **because he was hungry.**

John	*wa*	*onaka ga suite ita*	*node*
John	subject marker	was hungry	because

kukki	*o*	*tabemashita*
cookies	object marker	ate

3. The device of agglutination is a distinctive feature of the Japanese language, as with other Altaic languages. In an agglutinative language significant words or roots can be joined together in a string, with each part retaining its own form and meaning. English sometimes builds words in this way (un-tru-th-ful-ly), but Japanese builds phrases and sentences as follows:

tabe	*sase*	*rare*	*taku*
stem of verb "to eat"	causative form "cause to"	passive form	desiderative "want to"

na	*katta*
negative	past

These Japanese elements are agglutinated into one phrase:

35

Tabesaseraretakunakatta, which means "(I) did not want to be made to eat (that)."

Japanese phonology. Phonologically, the differences between English and Japanese are most evident in three areas: the vowels, the consonants, and other sound features such as stress and intonation.

1. *Vowel sounds.* English is known for its relatively complicated vowel system, while Japanese is noted for its simple, five-vowel system. English speakers who are acquainted with the Spanish language often remark that the five vowel sounds of Japanese are much like the five vowels in Spanish. On the list of English and Japanese vowels below, as written in the International Phonetic Alphabet, only one vowel sound can be said to be the "same" in the two languages. The following vowels usually give students of either second language the most difficulty in pronunciation. A native speaker of English will tend to say an English vowel sound within a Japanese word, and the Japanese speaker may likewise substitute a Japanese vowel sound in the middle of an English word. English has 15 vowel sounds, and Japanese has five vowel sounds, as the following illustrates:

English vowels   **Japanese vowels**

/iy/ as in **beat**
/I / as in **bit**   ⎤— similar sounds /i/ as in *iki* (breath)

/ey/ as in **bait**
/ɛ/ as in **bet**   ⎤— similar sounds /e/ as in *eki* (station)
/ae / as in **bat**

/a/ as in **pot** ——————— same sound /a/ as in *aki* (autumn)

/ ə / as in **but**

/ər/ as in **bird**

/ ɔ / as in **bought**

/ow/ as in **boat** ——————— similar sound /o/ as in *oki* (off shore)

/U/ as in **put**
/uw/ as in **boot**   ⎤— similar sounds /u/ as in *uki* (float)

/aw/ as in **bout**

/ay/ as in **bite**

/oy/ as in **boy**

Four distinctions in English vowel sounds are sometimes difficult for Japanese speakers to hear and to pronounce (especially for older learners). Special sensitivity and patience may be needed on the part of the staff while students learn to hear and produce the differences in these English sounds. Students soon will recognize that the meaning of two different English words often depends on one of these distinctions in vowel sounds.

First distinction between English vowel sounds:

/æ/ and /a/ and /ə/

rat	rot	rut
fan		fun
map	mop	
cat	cot	cut
lack	lock	luck

Second distinction between English vowel sounds:

/ɔ/ and /ow/

bought	boat
caught	coat
paltry	poultry

Third distinction between English vowel sounds:

/iy/ and /I/

beat	bit
sheep	ship
peek	pick

Fourth distinction between English vowel sounds:

/U/ and /uw/

soot	suit
look	luke

Many other subtle distinctions between Japanese vowel sounds and English vowel sounds are described by linguists, including many special features of Japanese vowels—such as vowel length—which English speakers find difficult to hear and master. But the four sets of vowel distinctions above account for the major differences encountered by the Japanese speaker who is learning English.

A final note about vowels: although the English-speaking student recites the vowels in the order a-e-i-o-u, the Japanese speaker has been taught the five vowels in the order a-i-u-e-o.

2. *Consonant sounds.* Speakers of both English and Japanese make use of particular consonant sounds that are not used in the other language. The English consonants that are new to the Japanese native speaker learning English will be discussed; however, the English speaker learning Japanese would encounter several distinctive consonant sounds in Japanese as well. The following English consonants do not occur in Japanese:

/f/ as in **f**eet
/v/ as in **v**enus
/ θ / as in **th**ief
/ ð / as in **th**ese
/l/ as in **l**ead
/r/ as in **r**ead
/z/ as in lei**s**ure

Learning new sounds requires learning new contrasts. The distinction between /l/ and /r/ is perhaps the most difficult one for Japanese, because the Japanese /ř/, a flap consonant, is pronounced just half way between the articulation of the /l/ and /r/ in English. Both /l/ and /r/ may sound exactly the same to the Japanese ear. The difference between /b/ and /v/ is usually not easy to master, and learning to pronounce /f/, / θ /, and / ð / is also a new exercise for the Japanese speaker.

Certain consonants are new for Japanese because of their distribution in English words. The Japanese /s/ does not occur before /i/; therefore, a Japanese native speaker might at first substitute /ši/ for /si/ in English words. The number six might be pronounced "shix."

Each Japanese consonant is always followed by a vowel: words never end in a consonant (the consonant /h/ is the only exception to this rule). When a Japanese speaker attacks an English word in which several consonants are unseparated by vowels, the tendency may be to sound out the word as if it were written in the *kana* pattern of consonant and vowel syllables. The English word "strike" might be sounded out as "su-to-rai-ku"; and "cream" might be pronounced as "kurimu." Such approaches occasionally reveal themselves in spelling errors.

3. *Language rhythms.* English is a language whose rhythm is based on stress: linguists agree that four different degrees of stress are functional in English. Japanese, on the contrary, has no stress. The most important feature of the Japanese prosody is the mora or the unit of duration. Japanese utterances are composed of morae and, consequently, Japanese speakers are very sensitive to the length of sounds. Japanese speakers must learn to recognize stress in learning English, just as English speakers must learn to hear the durational contrast among Japanese sounds.

Japanese words are marked by pitch accent, and there are many minimal pairs to illustrate the linguistic function of this feature. For example, the Japanese word *ame* can mean "rain" or "candy," depending on the pitch accent. However, in a practical sense, the differences in word accent do not pose serious problems to either Japanese speakers learning English or English speakers learning Japanese. There are diverse dialectical variations in word accent in Japanese, but these variations seldom interfere with communication among native speakers.

In Japan teachers of English traditionally have concentrated on reading and grammar and have given little attention to pronunciation. Because of this neglect of spoken English education in Japan and the wide gap between the phonological systems of English and Japanese, native speakers of Japanese who come to California schools may have a literary knowledge of English but may still need assistance first in hearing the distinctions among English sounds and rhythms and then in accurately producing natural-sounding English speech.

Characteristics of Japanese Written Language

Written Japanese consists of two phonetic sets of symbols, *hiragana* and *katakana,* plus a set of Chinese characters called *kanji,* all conventionally used within the same sentence or text. The two *kana* systems are the phonetic, or more properly phonemic, parts of the written language. Chinese characters are logographic; that is, they stand for a specific word rather than a sound.

Both systems of *kana, hiragana* and *katakana,* are called syllabaries rather than alphabets because each symbol represents a syllable. It is possible to transcribe anything from the spoken language into either of these two systems. In the middle ages several classics of Japanese literature were written entirely in *hiragana* by women who were not taught Chinese characters. Even today, telegrams within Japan are sent entirely in *katakana*. But these uses are exceptional. Each system of *kana* is used for specific functions within the written language.

The first system is the set of cursive-like figures called *hiragana*. By means of 48 figures, such as the following examples, plus several marks that indicate distinctions between voiced and voiceless sounds, any Japanese expression may be written down. With similar ease, anyone who has memorized the sound-symbol correlations of *hiragana* can readily decode this writing system, even without understanding the meaning:

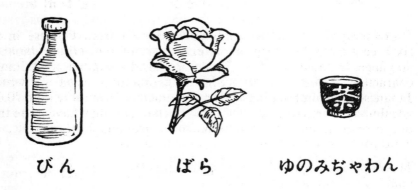

びん　　　　ばら　　　　ゆのみぢゃわん

Hiragana is used for completing the grammatical endings on words with stems that are represented by Chinese characters and for writing the grammatical particles that hold a Japanese sentence together. Some Japanese words traditionally have been written in *hiragana* only.

The second totally phonetic writing system used in Japanese corresponds to the same 48 sounds represented by *hiragana,* but in this second system, the graphic symbols seem more visually "squared off." This second system is called *katakana.*

In ordinary use *katakana,* is reserved for the transliteration of words and names from Western languages into Japanese. A map of the world, for example, will show the names of most countries in *katakana* transliterations, such as:

カ ナ ダ"　or　エ ク ア ド ル

KA NA DA　　　E KU A DO RU

(Canada)　　　　(Ecuador)

40

Other examples of the *katakana* syllabary are as follows:

ペン   ペリカン   ピンポン

Logographic characters, originally adopted from Chinese in the sixth century A.D., form an integral part of the written Japanese language. In Japanese, these figures are called *kanji,* literally "Chinese characters." About 2,000 *kanji* are commonly used in written Japanese, but combinations of these characters form more than 70,000 vocabulary words (Nelson, 1973). Each character may have more than one pronunciation and more than one meaning. For example, the word for "Japan" is written with two characters:

This is pronounced *Nihon* or *Nippon;* it is the name of the country of Japan.

Alone, the first character is pronounced *nichi* and means "sun." Another basic meaning, related to sun, is "day." In compounds this character may be pronounced *ni, hi,* or *bi.*

Alone, this character is pronounced *hon* when it means "book," or *moto* when it means "origin" or "source." In a compound this character may also be pronounced "hon" or "pon" or "moto."

Nihon may be written either across, from left to right, or down the page.

This is the character for person or people. This character has no other meaning. Alone, it is pronounced *hito,* but in compounds it is pronounced *bito, jin,* or *nin.*

All together, these three characters are pronounced *nihonjin,* and they mean "Japanese people" or "a Japanese." Only context will tell if this is singular or plural.

41

While most speakers of English initially find such a system of symbols with differing meanings and pronunciations to be quite confusing, even English writing contains many examples of such logographs that can change in their meaning or pronunciation. Most English speakers readily know the different meanings and pronunciations of the following "characters":

She handed the driver a $5.	(a five or a five-dollar bill)
Beethoven's 5th	(fifth)
Please send $$$!	(money or cash)

Japanese *kanji* comprise nouns, proper names, or the roots of modifiers and verbs. Because Japanese is a highly inflected language, unlike Chinese in which endings of words do not change for grammatical purposes, the Japanese had to invent a way of tacking various endings onto words to express their distinctions in tense, as in cook**ing,** cook**ed,** or cook**er.** For such a purpose, the syllabic *kana* system was developed in the early centuries to hold the characters together with grammatical parts. The typical Japanese sentence is made up of both *kanji* and *kana*, as follows:

日 本　　　から　　　来 ました。

Nihon	*kara*	*kimashita*
Japan	from	came

English translation: (I) came from Japan.

Although the Roman alphabet is not technically part of the Japanese writing system, it is used for special purposes in Japan. Words or phrases from English or another European language may be used to impart an exotic flair to advertisements or to decorate consumer goods. Sometimes, Japanese words are romanized to make a poster or a magazine cover eye-catching. Roman letters are called *romaji* in Japanese.

Japanese is sometimes transliterated into *romaji*. *Romaji* may be used in teaching the Japanese language to foreigners or in citing Japanese words and phrases in a Western publication, such as this handbook. Romanization may be necessary to express a Japanese person's name or place name in a way that can be read by Westerners. There are several systems of romanization in use; this book uses the Hepburn system.

An example of a page from a student's textbook, illustrating the use of *hiragana, katakana,* and *kanji,* is shown in Figure 1.

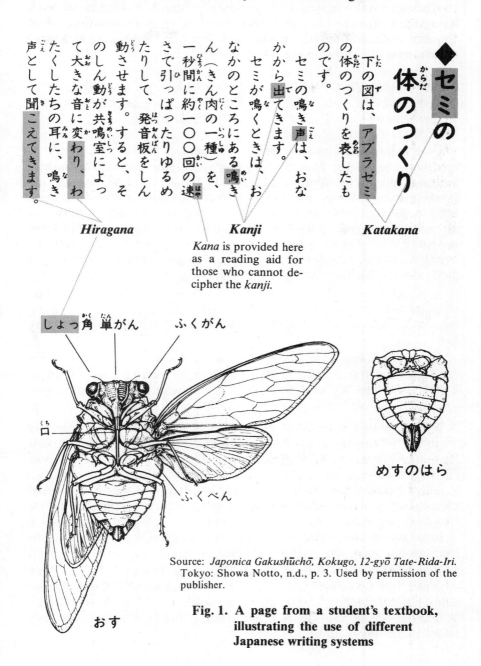

◆セミの
体のつくり

下の図は、アブラゼミの体のつくりを表したものです。

セミの鳴き声は、おなかから出てきます。

セミが鳴くときは、おなかのところにある鳴き（きん肉の一種）を、一秒間に約一〇〇回の速さで引っぱったりゆるめたりして、発音板をしん動させます。すると、そのしん動が共鳴室によって大きな音に変わり、わたくしたちの耳に、鳴き声として聞こえてきます。

Hiragana **Kanji** **Katakana**

Kana is provided here as a reading aid for those who cannot decipher the *kanji.*

しょっ角　単がん　ふくがん

口

ふくべん

めすのはら

おす

Source: *Japonica Gakushūchō, Kokugo, 12-gyō Tate-Rida-Iri.* Tokyo: Showa Notto, n.d., p. 3. Used by permission of the publisher.

Fig. 1. A page from a student's textbook, illustrating the use of different Japanese writing systems

Introduction of the Language Systems

Hiragana is taught first to young children. Many children learn *hiragana* at home or in kindergarten before entering the first grade. Reading and writing lessons in the first grade are taught primarily through the use of *hiragana.*

Katakana is introduced to first graders, and practice may continue in the second grade. The rules of orthography for *katakana* differ slightly from those of *hiragana,* so students continue to master these in the primary school years. As students encounter more sophisticated foreign-loan words in the upper-grade levels, they learn to recognize and write more and more words in *katakana.*

Kanji is introduced in the first grade; at each subsequent level in elementary school, a given number of new *kanji* characters are prescribed in the national curriculum. In textbooks for each grade level, only the *kanji* symbols that are appropriate to that grade level are used. *Hiragana* is used for words that are recognized aurally but are not yet prescribed in *kanji.*

First graders learn 76 characters, second graders learn 145 characters, third graders learn 195 characters, and so on. In six years of elementary school, students learn to read and write about 1,000 characters. These are called the "characters for daily use"; a person who uses these is functionally literate for most demands of everyday life.

Junior high school students continue to learn *kanji* at each grade level; they learn to recognize, if not write from memory, an additional 1,000 characters. With this total of 2,000 characters, junior high school graduates can read most modern publications and works of literature.

Senior high school students continue to use the same 2,000 *kanji* in new combinations for more advanced vocabulary and continue to learn archaic or rare characters used in old literature or historical references.

The Roman alphabet is first introduced to students in the upper elementary years. In elementary school *romaji* is taught for simple purposes such as addressing an envelope or romanizing one's name. Formal foreign language instruction begins in the first year of junior high school, using the Roman alphabet.

Please refer to Chapter IV for a discussion of the actual teaching of *kana* and *kanji* to students and to Appendix C for the Japanese national curriculum concerning the teaching of *kana* and *kanji.* Appendix C also includes a graph of *kanji* taught at each grade level of an elementary school.

Interrelationship Between Language and Culture

Several features of the structure and usage of the Japanese language seem distinctly "different" to Americans, so it is natural to try to understand these features as a part of the overall Japanese cultural scheme. Of course, if such differences say something about the Japanese culture, then they also speak about American language and culture. By considering the different forms and functions of a language such as Japanese in relation to the culture of Japan, we can enrich our understanding of many interrelated structures within language and culture that we take for granted every day.

Levels of Politeness

In both the vocabulary and grammar of Japanese, various levels of politeness are available to the speaker. Depending on the relative status and the direction of the action involving the person speaking, the person spoken to, and the person or thing spoken about, the speaker may choose different words and forms to express the sentence. For many of the basic verbs, such as "give," "receive," "do," "say," "come," and "know," at least two Japanese words are available, each imparting a different status to the subject or the object of the verb. Each verb in Japanese is further transformed by a choice of endings, each option adding the same grammatical information (such as verb tense) but carrying different levels of politeness or deference. Many nouns that refer to household or kinship concepts also have a plain version and an honorific version. Thus, when talking about one's own house, a speaker will say *uchi,* the plain word for "house," but when referring to the house of a friend in conversation, the speaker will use *o-taku,* the honorific word for "house." This system of honorific speech has several implications.

First, to a great extent, honorific speech in Japanese serves the function performed by pronouns in English. Since the polite verb for "go" is used in face-to-face conversation to mean "(you) go," and the humble verb for "go" is used to mean "(I) go," the subject or reference is always clear without being explicitly stated by the use of a pronoun. Likewise, *o-taku* can mean only "your house" and *uchi* can mean only "my house," so no possessive pronouns are needed to modify either word for "house." Although the Japanese language does not use pronouns in the same way as English, there are other ways of referring to "I," "me," "you," "your," "he," "his," and so on. In polite speech, however, these terms are avoided as much as possible. It is especially bad form to use "you" or "your" when speaking directly to a person who commands respect, such as a teacher. If necessary, the speaker will refer to the teacher as though in the third person: "Will the teacher go, too?" meaning "Will you go, too?"

The Japanese speaker who is new to a California setting and just learning English may grope for ways to be polite in the new language. The natural recourse is to avoid using pronouns such as "you" and "I" and to look for distinctions among synonyms that can lend more politeness to speech. Of course, because vocabulary is relatively undifferentiated in English (everybody simply "goes" and a "house" is a "house" whether it is mine or yours), the use of pronouns is essential. The natural usage of English pronouns with verbs and nouns undistinguished in politeness level may need to be modeled and reinforced for native speakers of Japanese. Likewise, while "residence" is a more formal word than "house," its use in conversation ("Where is your residence?") sounds simply more stilted than polite. To help the Japanese native speaker to feel comfortable in English, speakers of English can model and practice natural usage, steering the student away from artificially formal English. Methods of adding politeness are to be found in English usage, but certainly not by a direct application of the distinctions that are found in Japanese.

Another implication of the importance of politeness levels in Japanese is that in speaking Japanese, improper word choice or verb inflection may constitute a social breach. A speaker may inadvertently insult the listener by the wrong choice of speech forms. (In fact, deliberate insults in Japanese are often quite innocuous in content but simply couched in terms used to speak "down" to inferiors or in terms extravagantly formal.) Coming from this background, Japanese speakers may be doubly reluctant to make mistakes in English. Japanese students and their parents who are hesitant about speaking English as a second language might well be reassured that grammatical mistakes in English rarely constitute a personal affront.

One of the important goals of primary language development in a Japanese bilingual classroom will be the preservation of respect for and the development of mastery in the use of politeness levels in Japanese conversation. A common reflection among Japanese-American students who are taking up the study of Japanese in their college years is that, although they learned to speak Japanese on the intimate and informal politeness levels used by children in the home, they never learned the proper command of politeness levels that would enable them to speak confidently as adults outside the family setting. In the normal language development of children in Japan, politeness levels are mastered by the time students reach the junior high school years. Thus, while even a six-year-old Japanese-speaking child knows all the basic vocabulary and syntax of Japanese, the child will just be starting the important transition from the informal style of children's speech to the distinctions in politeness level and style that characterize competent adult speech. If primary language development is interrupted between the ages of six and twelve, the aspect of speech most likely to be sacrificed will be the capacity to use politeness levels in Japanese.

Distinctions Between Male and Female Speech

Another feature of the Japanese language that Americans find related to culture is the difference in the vocabulary and the politeness levels used by male and female speakers. While some linguists insist that such differences characterize language use between the sexes even in English (Lakoff, 1975), the differences in vocabulary and form in English are not as clearly marked as in Japanese. Distinctions in speech styles begin to form even among schoolchildren in the primary grades. Differences are more observable in the informal speech among men friends and among women friends than in formal speech situations; even in formal speech, however, many features of language use differ. Japanese language textbooks available to Westerners often present only the more polite end of the possibilities in Japanese speech, a realm predominantly used by women. Thus, men's speech in Japan is difficult for the Western student to understand, since the forms have not been presented in textbooks or tapes. Moreover, when Western men arrive in Japan speaking good textbook Japanese, they are sometimes laughed at in good humor as "talking like women."

Modeling of typical speech of both men and women in English and Japanese will be important in developing a natural speech style among bilingual boys and girls and in developing a receptive understanding of the styles that are distinctive to the speech of both men and women in Japanese.

Avoidance of the Word "No"

In the midst of a great cultural emphasis on harmony and respect in Japan, one speaker will rarely directly contradict another or even answer a question with a direct "no." Even in situations in which Americans can perceive "nothing personal" to be conveyed by a "no" answer, the Japanese will usually find one of at least 16 different ways of saying "no" without using the literal equivalent, *iie* (Ueda, 1974). Conventionally, even questions in Japanese are phrased in such a way to allow the respondent to avoid saying no. When the native speaker of Japanese learns that the translation for *iie* is the English word "no," the individual may ascribe to the English "no" all the blunt and inelegant sensations which *iie* may carry. Thus, a second-language strategy may be to search for ways to avoid using the word "no," even while intending to convey a negative answer. School staff can be careful to listen for implicit "no" answers rather than direct ones, can phrase open-ended questions rather than questions that require a possible "no" answer, and can model friendly and natural ways of saying "no" in English.

Answers to Negatively Phrased Questions

A further complication in asking questions requiring an affirmative or negative answer is that Japanese speakers and English speakers tend to respond in opposite ways for the same meaning. The Japanese speaker responds to the literal sense of the question, while the English speaker gives a "yes" or a "no" in relation to the context. For example, a teacher asks a question of a student who does not have a pencil:

Teacher: You don't have a pencil?
American student: No. (Meaning no, I don't have a pencil.)
Japanese student: Yes. (Meaning yes, as you said, I don't have a pencil.)

To avoid any misunderstanding when the issue is important, the English-speaking teacher can avoid negatively phrased questions or phrase the question another way. This structure can be worked on in both the English-as-a-second-language component and in the Japanese language development component. When both the speaker and listener are conscious of this pitfall, misunderstandings can be avoided.

Use of Personal Names in Japanese

Japanese names are written with the family name first and the given name second, as in *Kawamura Kenji.*

(family name) (given name)

Middle names are not used in the Japanese language. Most Japanese will realize that the order of family name and given name is reversed in English, and they will often use the English order whenever they write their names in *romaji,* the Roman alphabet. In English-speaking cultures a personal signature often is required to make a document official, but in Japan individuals make their mark for all the same purposes with a small, carved name-seal stamped in red ink.

In Japan given names are used primarily by parents when they talk to their children or by older family friends when they speak to or about the children. Children within the family must call elder brothers and sisters by respectful terms and may call only younger siblings by their given names. By the time students are in junior high school, they are in the habit of calling each other by school nicknames or by their family names, as is the adult practice throughout Japan. Rarely do friends, young couples in courtship, or even husbands and wives use each other's given names.

48

In Japan students commonly refer to their teacher as simply *sensei,* rather than Mr. Kawamoto, for example. Similarly, recent immigrant students may also address their American teacher with the English equivalent of "Teacher," rather than Ms. Jones. Teachers should interpret this short form of address as a problem in generalizing from Japanese to English, not as a grammatical error or sign of disrespect.

In the American school setting, Japanese high school students might be surprised or embarrassed to hear their given names used by their teachers. Likewise, parents who recently have arrived from Japan would not expect to be called by their first names by school personnel. Nor would they themselves expect to use the first name of a teacher or principal. Of course, part of the cultural experience in California is adjusting oneself to different definitions of formality at school and elsewhere. In this respect the school staff can help the Japanese newcomer student and parents to understand American name usage and to agree mutually on what everyone may call each other. Japanese-style name usage can be modeled and reinforced in Japanese language activities for all students.

It is important for people to make every effort to pronounce Japanese names clearly and completely. Given their polysyllabic character, one easily can drop a syllable off here or there unintentionally. With practice, however, it will become easy to give every syllable its proper emphasis when calling the students' names.

Standardized National Language

One feature of the Japanese language that might reflect the relatively homogeneous identity of the island nation is that the language itself falls under the care of the Ministry of Education, which standardizes and periodically revises the acceptable usage and writing of Japanese. Even the characters that may be used legally for given names, for example, are determined by the central language bureau. Conformity to these standards is the responsibility of the bureaucracy, the national media, and the educational system at all levels.

Nonverbal Behaviors That Affect Learning

Many differences exist in the customary nonverbal messages among speakers of Japanese and English. Native speakers of both languages usually enjoy discussing the differences in gestures and expressions that are integral to the two languages and cultures. Bilingual teachers can incorporate questions such as the following into language activities to encourage understanding among students who are learning both verbal and nonverbal conventions of the two languages:

1. What gesture means "me" in Japanese and in English? (Japanese point to their nose; Americans point to their chest.)

2. What gesture means "no" in Japanese and in English? (Japanese wave one hand in front of the face; Americans move the head from side to side.)
3. What happens when a person sneezes and sniffles with a cold? (Americans will chorus "Gesundheit" or some such blessing, but Japanese say nothing to focus attention on the poor sneezer. In Japanese behavior, it is rude to blow one's nose in front of others, but Americans think it's poor form to keep sniffling.)
4. What do the animals "say" in Japanese and English? (Japanese dogs say wan-wan, while American dogs say bow-wow, and so on.)

Bilingual teachers and students should be able to think of other examples to add to the list. Only a few general areas of nonverbal cultural differences that are most likely to influence understanding among the students will be considered in this section.

Standards of Comportment

In the physical behavior of a student vis-à-vis adults, certain traditional Japanese expectations may be open to misunderstanding in the American setting. While Americans have been conditioned to believe that a smile or eye-to-eye contact best represents one in public, at a fairly young age the Japanese person is taught to feel that he or she is best represented by a serious expression and a bowed head. Students project a solemn expression in their school photographs in Japan, while their American counterparts are saying "cheese." Students in Japan still stand up and bow in unison when the teacher enters the room and sometimes rise to address the teacher. Touching between teacher and student is rare beyond the primary grades, eye contact is fleeting, and the student's expression in responding to the teacher is usually serious. The challenge to the American viewer is to see in these conventions neither a lack of warmth nor a loss of communication but to accept these behaviors as a sign of cooperativeness from the newcomer student from Japan. Staff and fellow students can help the newcomer student practice new conventions, such as shaking hands, sustaining eye contact, smiling at the audience, and so on.

Dealing with Numbers

Students in Japan acquire habits of dealing with numbers that are much different from the ways in which Americans learn to manipulate numbers. To count from one to ten on the fingers, a Japanese will use only the right hand. Starting with the hand fully open and palm up, the fingers are folded in to lie on the palm (thumb first) to count from one to five. Then they are unfolded in reverse order (from the little finger back to the thumb) to continue counting from six through ten. A Japanese student will hold up just the thumb to signify "one" and will find it strange that the American teacher uses the index finger to indicate "one."

The forms by which Japanese students learn to say their multiplication tables and to work out arithmetic problems on paper are slightly different from the systems taught in American schools. A Japanese newcomer student might know how to get the right answer, but his or her way of solving the division problem, for example, might mystify the American teacher. On the other side of the coin, the Japanese father may have trouble helping his child to deal with fractions the "American" way, since the procedures in the American textbook may be quite strange to parents who went to school in Japan.

Another convention involving numbers that sometimes causes confusion is the use of a different system of counting years of age in Japan. Until recently a child was considered to be one year old during the first year of life (from birth to twelve months), two years old during the second year of life (from twelve to twenty-four months), and so on, making the child seem one year older than the American child born on the same date. Although this practice is now less common in Japan, it may still cause an occasional misunderstanding about the age of a Japanese newcomer student.

When the American registrar asks about the year of a Japanese student's birth, another difference in dating may reveal itself. With the reign of each emperor in Japan, a new calendar era is named in which the years begin again from one. In 1986 we are in the sixty-first year of the reign of the present emperor, whose era is known as *Shōwa*. Thus, 1986 is known within Japan as *Shōwa* 61, the year 1987 will be *Shōwa* 62, and so on. Adults in Japan know how to convert the *Shōwa* year to the Western calendar year, but a Japanese child might know only that he or she was born in the year *Shōwa* 49, with no clue that this was 1974 to the American mind.

Offering and Declining

In traditional Japan, which is deeply influenced by Confucian virtues, many social rituals demonstrating humility, reticence, respect, and generosity often dominate personal feelings and expression, particularly with such an important figure as one's teacher. Americans, more accustomed to assuming that personal feeling are the bases of all outward behavior, are unlikely to question the authenticity of a person's gestures or statements or are less apt to view them as having ritualistic rather than literal meaning. In this respect the acts of

51

extending, accepting, and declining offers or invitations are understood differently in Japan and in the United States. The general rule in Japan is that the first offer is an important ritualistic gift of words, but it is not necessarily to be taken literally. Only an offer that is made several times or only a repeated "No, thank you" is to be accepted as the true, literal will of the speaker. This difference from the American habit (of taking the first offer or the first decline at face value) has implications for persons who are learning to be "bicultural" and for promoting understanding among students in the American classroom.

In bridging this cultural difference, a Japanese person usually learns to be careful of the offers one makes or declines when speaking to an American, because one's statements are likely to be understood at literal face value once and for all. The American, at the same time, learns to feel thankful for a generous offer from a Japanese but to decline the offer the first time, on the understanding that it is truly the "thought" in the case that counts. Only with repeated offers or several urging invitations will the American know that the offer is a literal one on the part of the Japanese person. The American will likewise understand that a Japanese may politely decline the first invitation, but that, if the invitation is repeated several times, it will be understood to be serious and may be accepted gladly after all.

In the classroom this syndrome may take many forms that seem quite small in themselves, but that may impede communication between the American teacher and the Japanese newcomer student. The teacher's first question, "Do you understand?" may be met with a "Yes" from the student who has not understood a thing. The implicit offer of help from the teacher may have to be repeated several times by the teacher before it is perceived by the student as a genuine willingness to go over the material again. The Japanese newcomer student or parent may at first seem hesitant to join in some activity or to accept any form of outreach or offer on the part of the teacher, but repeated invitations will make the offer clearly genuine and literal. Even an offer of a cup of coffee may be declined by the Japanese parent until it is offered a second or third time. The Japanese mother may have to be invited several times to participate in a class activity or to demonstrate some aspect of Japanese culture to the class in order to overcome her deference, humility, or assumption that the invitation is just a social formality on the part of the teacher.

Thus, even while the level of conversation may be verbal, many nonverbal conventions are operative at all times in English and in Japanese, and it will be these subtle modes of understanding that will require the most attention from teachers and students who are learning to communicate in two linguistic and cultural styles.

Chapter IV

Recommended Instructional and Curricular Strategies for Japanese Language Development

Research on students of many language backgrounds strongly supports an affirmative effort by the school to cultivate each student's potential bilinguality. This approach will have rewards not only for Japanese skills levels but also for English skills levels and academic achievement. When the alternative—no attention to Japanese language development—makes the school a party to Japanese language loss and to cognitive stagnation, the choice of most schools and parents is for sustained development of Japanese language skills in the academic setting.

The California school that wishes to provide Japanese language development to Japanese-speaking students has several advantages. Usually, one or more adults in each LEP student's home are able to read and write Japanese. They should be asked to work with the student at home in support of school activities. Some parents or grandparents might be willing to work with students in the school setting itself. In the large urban areas, a community Japanese school may provide Japanese instruction on Saturdays. Materials for reading and teaching Japanese are easily available at specialty bookstores in San Francisco and Los Angeles. The Ministry of Education of Japan and the schools for overseas Japanese in the large urban areas will be happy to share information with public schools that enroll Japanese-speaking LEP students. California has many resource centers that provide information about Japan and about Japanese Americans. Finally, because of the long history of immigration from Japan to California, almost every community has people who are bilingual and bicultural and who can help to advise the school about positive programs for both Japanese-American students and Japanese newcomer students who may be in the U.S. only a few years.

After investigating relationships between Japanese language maintenance and other variables in a student's environment in the U.S., Fumiko Okamoto-Bichard (1985) reported that high skills in both Japanese and English were correlated most strongly with two factors. The first was the emotional satisfaction and outlook of the student, or the degree to which the student was enjoying his or her present schooling. The second was the amount of time spent using and listening to each language. All of the students in this study attended a Saturday school for Japanese overseas children, and 80 percent of their parents held high expectations that their children would learn both languages well; however, some students did well in only one language, while others did poorly in both languages. In conclusion, Saturday school and the expectations of parents by themselves do not ensure maintenance of the Japanese language. The public school should play a vital role in building emotional support for the student's own outlook about being a bilingual and bicultural individual. At the same time, the public school should provide maximum exposure to both languages.

Readiness Skills

The readiness of both the student and the school staff must be considered before Japanese language development activities are introduced in the classroom. The actual teaching of Japanese reading and writing should then be successful. The timing of the introduction of English instruction and the relation between the two strands of language development will require thoughtful planning. But if the goal of "additive bilingualism" is maintained while instruction in both Japanese and English is continuing, the rewards for the school and for the students should be both immediate and long-term.

Five skills are necessary before reading and writing in Japanese can begin. The first two requisites for learning to read and write in Japanese are the same visual skills and sensorimotor coordination that English-speaking children need to begin reading. These are nonlanguage-specific skills, but they are learned through the use of language, such as naming basic shapes, comparing same and different, and counting in order.

The next two required skills are a command of spoken Japanese and a knowledge of concepts by which the student can begin to understand and analyze meanings in the written language. Oral language development in Japanese can build both these skills at the same time. The fifth requisite for beginning to read and write is motivation.

These five skills are discussed in the remainder of this section. Some classroom activities are suggested.

Visual Skills

Visual skills include recognizing basic shapes, sizes, and colors; telling whether patterns are the same or different; naming the items that are missing in a picture; and choosing the picture that is different from the others. Some children are rehearsed in these skills by parents before entering school; however, training should continue toward finer visual distinctions at the preschool, kindergarten, and primary levels of school. These abilities are required before a person can learn to read in Japanese or in English.

Sensorimotor Skills

The motor control skills and eye-hand coordination skills necessary to begin writing are called sensorimotor skills. A sequence of activities usually leads from the gross-motor level to the fine-motor level and from the three-dimensional space around the body to the two-dimensional area of the page. First, isolated motions are mastered, such as jumping, throwing, catching, and clapping. Second, sustained sequences of actions related to a whole task are required; for example, acting out all the body motions that accompany a song or cutting and pasting pieces of paper to make a picture. Finally, the hands and fingers practice the fine skills of handling crayons, paper, and pencil. Prewriting pencil-and-paper practice may include drawing lines through a maze, drawing basic shapes such as circles and triangles, and making Xs or Os on work sheets in response to visual discrimination tasks.

The visual and sensorimotor skills that are required to begin reading in Japanese may be developed by the same techniques used with children who are beginning to read in English. Instruction in the Japanese language, however, is essential to the students' learning of the names of the shapes and the colors and the concepts of same and different that are entailed in visual discrimination tasks. Prereading work sheets for practice in matching, differentiating, connecting the dots, tracing, or coloring should be reviewed with an eye to culturally specific concepts before Japanese newcomer children are asked to complete them. However, large-motor activities and rhythmic activities can be introduced to all the children. The Japanese children's game of *Jan-ken-po,* known in English as "Rock-Scissors-Paper," can be taught to all students as an exercise in rhythm, quick observation, and logical mental calculation. Exercises in music can include Japanese songs as well as English songs. Japanese children often first learn to distinguish the units of the *kana* syllabary through songs, because each note of a song usually requires one syllable of *kana.* Crafts can include activities such as Japanese *origami* (paper folding), kite making, or cutting and pasting the cherry blossoms or red maple leaves that mark the change of seasons in Japan. These crosscultural activities for prereaders are easy to design for primary-level students. Such activities also can be used by all students for improving their visual and sensorimotor skills.

Students who have learned to read in Japanese before entering a California classroom will not need to repeat these stages of prereading skills development in the Japanese reading strand. The oral English development strand, however, may include English vocabulary and sentence patterns for the same tasks of counting, naming, comparing big and small, and so on.

Oral Language Skills

Students need personal mastery of most of the sounds, syntax, and common vocabulary of spoken Japanese before they can begin to read and write. Exposure to many kinds of oral language styles should increase the oral language preparedness of students who hear Japanese only from their mothers. By means of films or videos and stories read aloud, teachers and classroom guests can model for young children the different levels of polite and formal speech used outside the home. By listening to stories, songs, or poems in Japanese, the students should become aware of the various styles of Japanese language reading materials. The students should practice using the various styles of language in their own writing.

Conceptual Skills

Conceptual skills include the abilities to organize thoughts in chronological or thematic order, to anticipate consequences, to explain similarities and differences, to classify things, to give simple definitions, and to identify difficult words or phenomena. Development of these skills involves building awareness of surroundings, feelings, people's roles and relations, and many life experiences. As students practice these analytical skills through play, word games, and informal discussions, they prepare themselves for the conceptual demands of reading and writing. Vocabulary is a reflection of concepts, and the school program should include a broad range of experiences to prepare students for the concepts and vocabulary of the reading material. The California school must actively fill the gaps between the immediate American world of the students and the Japanese cultural world that is assumed in reading materials that come from Japan.

Oral language and cultural concepts can be presented simultaneously in the classroom. Japanese stories can be read aloud. Students of different levels of proficiency in Japanese and English can collaborate in telling stories to the class in both languages or in acting out the parts of Japanese folktales like *Momotaro* (Peach Boy). The earliest stories that youngsters encounter in Japanese readers contain references to many culturally specific things and practices. Children in California may or may not know about the dragonflies and shaved ice confections that fill a typical Japanese child's summer or the *tengu* (a kind of troll) and tortoises that inhabit the fantasy realms in Japanese children's literature. Japanese-speaking students should be given opportunities to speak with adults at school who understand Japanese. They should be allowed to listen to an adult model of Japanese, to speak to persons outside the family, and to discuss freely their questions and feelings that they may not be able to express in English.

The school must introduce to the students a new realm of "academic" oral language that is necessary both for becoming a fluent reader of Japanese and for acquiring a fully developed adult command of oral Japanese. The student must learn to follow abstract explanations and be able to express the same. Public speaking or reporting requires a formal and polite style, which the school must help to develop as students reach the upper elementary and junior high school grades. Oral language development and concept development are not exercises that stop with a minimal level of reading readiness; they must continue in parallel with more advanced literacy skills throughout the school years.

Motivation for Reading and Writing

Motivation to read and write in Japanese at school can be promoted through an environment that is rich in opportunities, reading materials, and encouragement from all teachers and students. The teachers and the principal of the school must communicate the goals of the school program to the students' parents. In addition, school personnel should coordinate their efforts with those of the staff of any supplementary Japanese school so that the school, home, and community programs support each other in encouraging language development. If other students show an interest in the Japanese language, their curiosity can be fostered to accord some prestige to the Japanese language-development activities for native speakers. Second-language learning circles for all students and native-language development for all students (in English, Japanese, Korean, Spanish, and so on) will provide an atmosphere in which both activities are "normal," not "different."

Students may be motivated by the satisfaction of reading stories, textbooks, and magazines in Japanese; by new possibilities of communicating through letters with friends or family far away; or by the rewards of contributing to group projects by way of information researched in Japanese. If Japanese reading lessons are coordinated with social studies lessons, for example, students might work in bilingual teams on a California history project by researching, writing, reporting, and making visual aids in both languages. Through such interface with other parts of the school curriculum, students' motivation for improving their Japanese language and reading skills can be supported throughout the grade levels.

Oral Language Skills

In the educational setting in Japan, all students have had six years of oral language development before entering first grade, where formal reading instruction begins. In California the preschool Japanese-speaking child may not be surrounded by the intensity of language experiences that would be common in Japan. The number of relatives and friends that speak to the child, the chances to listen to adults speaking normally among themselves, the hours of contact with Japanese-speaking playmates, and exposure to Japanese on radio and television may be limited, depending on the home and community circumstances. If this is the case, opportunities to speak Japanese with adults and other children at school will be especially valuable for reading readiness. Given normal development of oral language and cognitive skills, Japanese-speaking students should benefit from prereading instruction beginning in kindergarten and reading instruction beginning in the first grade.

Students' oral proficiency should match the difficulty level of the reading materials. Other than material published in Japan, there are few sequential, developmental reading series available for speakers of Japanese in the United States (see Appendix B). The school staff must choose and prepare early reading materials that are appropriate to the California setting and experiences of the students.

The conditions that affect preschool children's Japanese language development in California also affect the language growth of older students. That is, the amount of Japanese that the student hears in the community, home, and school may be more limited than would be the case in Japan. Therefore, the school must create opportunities for students to hear and speak Japanese at increasingly adult-like levels so that older students are continually prepared for more advanced reading materials.

Literacy Development in English

Many skills involved in reading and writing in Japanese can be directly transferred to literacy development in English. Students who are literate in Japanese are likely to be very efficient learners of English reading.

Students who have learned to read and write in Japanese can apply their eye-and-hand coordination to the physical task of reading and writing so that prereading skills do not have to be learned again. Furthermore, students who have learned to read and write in Japanese have a great stock of analytical vocabulary and cognitive skills that they can apply to reading English. They will understand that written language is a code and that there are particular rules for decoding (reading) and encoding (writing) to relate the spoken to the written language. Because these students have developed the habit of memorizing *kanji* through repetition, they can apply this practice to the memorization of English vocabulary and spelling.

Japanese-literate students will understand that the written page is structured by conventions of punctuation and layout and that knowledge of these conventions helps interpret the written material. They may be quick to analyze the nature of a document from physical clues (this is a letter, this is a poem, here is the author's name, here is the table of contents, and so on) even before they can fully comprehend the meaning of the sentences in English.

Japanese-literate students will know how to read for meaning— to seek the basic facts in a reading passage. Their success in transferring this skill to English reading will depend on knowledge of specific English vocabulary and syntax. When a Japanese-literate student encounters a point of difficulty in an English reading passage, many research and problem-solving skills will be transferred from the Japanese training: identifying the unknown words, seeking clues elsewhere in the context or the content of the passage, consulting a dictionary or other reference material, and describing a problem to the teacher.

Higher-level reading and writing skills in Japanese are analogous to those introduced gradually to native speakers of English: aesthetic appreciation of the features of literature and critical reading of nonfiction. These skills will be transferred to the study of English at the upper-grade levels.

In summary, although the surface features of Japanese and English are different, the concepts and the purposes of reading and writing are similar. The student who is literate in one language has many skills and a knowledge about language that can be applied readily to the challenge of learning to read and write in the other language. By dividing reading skills into the four categories of readiness, decoding, comprehension, and critical reading, Ada (1980) shows that most literacy skills are transferable from one language to another. Thus, she argues, "no one learns to read twice."

Planning a Japanese Reading Program

Although not everyone on the school staff can evaluate the readiness of the students for Japanese language instruction, all classroom teachers and administrators can take part in the discussion of "school readiness." No school can prepare a completely satisfactory Japanese-language instructional strand all at once out of thin air; each program must start in a developmental way. And, before a school can initiate a new language instructional program, the school's goals and commitments must be evaluated.

Different approaches within the school are possible with different concentrations of students. For example, Table 1 in Appendix A shows 32 districts enrolling more than 23 Japanese-speaking LEP students in 1986. In addition, about 50 districts enroll between ten and 50 students, and nearly 200 districts have ten or fewer students. Thus, realistically, Japanese reading instruction may take place in settings ranging from a "bilingual classroom" to broom-closet-variety individual assistance. Size, however, is not necessarily linked to quality of the school's program; through good planning and constant attention to building on-site resources, the school with only a few students may prove just as creative and effective as the school with many Japanese-speaking students.

At the point of beginning or upgrading Japanese language development activities, the school might look to the other kinds of first-language instruction provided in the community. Most districts that enroll Japanese-speaking students also have students who speak other languages. Bilingual education classes for other language groups in the school should contribute to the development of the Japanese reading instructional program. Experience with various management strategies may guide the teaching staff in structuring the Japanese component, and an environment in which many students are learning both their first language and a second language can increase the enthusiasm that Japanese-speaking students have for their Japanese studies.

Before a group of students is placed with an instructor of Japanese, each administrator, each school, and perhaps the district as a whole will want to review familiar planning questions, such as those in the following checklist. This checklist can be used for planning and for the continual evaluation of the Japanese language development strand. It should prove useful for administrators, teachers, bilingual teachers, aides, tutors, parents, and students.

Identifying the Students

1. How many students will benefit from Japanese reading instruction that assumes native-speaking ability?
2. Will some students want instruction in Japanese as a second language?
3. Are students who speak Japanese from Japan?
4. Are they likely to return to Japan in a few years?
5. How many speakers of Japanese have been raised in America, and what is the degree of their knowledge of Japan?
6. Is there any other school in the community that is providing academic instruction in Japanese, in Japanese as a second language, or in Japanese culture and arts?
7. How will the public school program work together with the community schools?

Developing Instructional Resources

1. Can school personnel teach Japanese reading?
2. Are community volunteers available to teach Japanese reading?
3. How will the school upgrade the skills of personnel to teach Japanese?
4. How will the school communicate with the parents of Japanese-speaking children and involve those parents in the language program and other school activities?
5. What materials can the school buy or borrow to improve Japanese language instruction?
6. How will space and time resources be allocated to Japanese language instruction?
7. How will Japanese reading be scheduled in the school day?

Achieving Goals and Policies

1. To what extent will language education in the school parallel education in the Japanese curriculum in Japan?
2. How will the Japanese language education curriculum be tailored to the California classroom and community?
3. How will materials be selected or created to reflect the above decisions?
4. Will progress through the Japanese language strand and the English language strand have contingencies related to each other?
5. How will the Japanese reading program relate to the other bilingual education programs in the school?
6. By what means will teachers and parents consult about the progress of students and discuss improvements in the curriculum?

With continual attention to such questions as these, even the school with limited resources can build toward an effective and well-integrated reading program for Japanese-speaking students.

Methods for Teaching Reading in Japanese

Teaching Japanese reading to students who speak Japanese is a relatively straightforward activity that requires a Japanese-literate adult with some teaching or tutoring experience, Japanese language materials geared to appropriate levels of reading and writing instruction, and sufficient time. If these resources are chosen and prepared in accordance with the students' needs and program goals identified by the school, then the actual reading lessons are likely to be quite simple and successful.

Among teachers in Japan there is little debate about approaches to reading instruction. The school does not have a "reading specialist" teacher. Class size is about 40 students even in the primary grades, and classrooms function without instructional aides or volunteers; so there is little individualization of reading lessons. In all elementary schools in Japan, students use the same basic reading and writing textbooks, and they progress through the textbooks at nearly the same rate in every classroom. Reading lessons at all the elementary grade levels consist of two main parts: (1) a passage of text for reading; and (2) an explanation of new vocabulary, *kanji,* and points of grammar for memorization and writing practice.

Hiragana

Young children usually are taught first to read *hiragana.* The written symbols are introduced with their corresponding sounds, which first

Source: *Benkyō Ichinensei Hiragana.* Tokyo: Shōgakkan, 1983, p. 28. Used by permission of the publisher.

must be read out loud by the teacher. Workbooks for the earliest grade levels contain pictorial examples of words that begin with each symbol of the *hiragana* syllabary. Each of the 48 *hiragana* symbols is introduced, as in the preceding example for the syllable *so*. In this picture, *so* is for *sora* (sky), *soto* (outside), *soko* (warehouse), *sora-tobuenban* (flying saucer), and so on.

Students learn to write *hiragana* one symbol at a time by following the large motions of the teacher's strokes on the chalkboard. They learn the correct starting point and order of strokes in each symbol; then they practice writing the whole symbol many times over within squared lines in their workbooks. The following example shows the syllable *ta*. Students learn to write the strokes in 1-2-3-4 order by writing over the faintly printed lines in the squares. The two diacritical marks (called *nigori*) at the upper-right corner of the *ta* make it voiced as *da*.

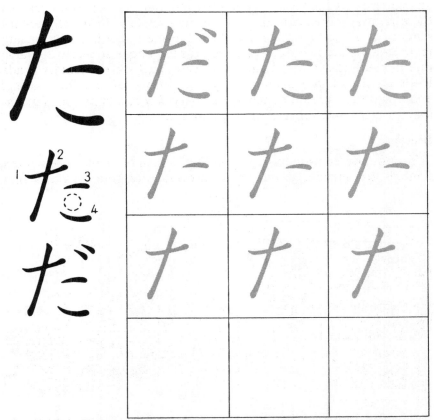

Source: *Benkyō Ichinensei Hiragana*. Tokyo: Shōgakkan, 1983, p. 29. Used by permission of the publisher,

The resources needed for learning *hiragana* are an introductory workbook and squared copy paper. These materials are available at specialty bookstores such as Kinokuniya in Los Angeles and San Francisco. (See Appendix B.)

While the students are learning *hiragana*, the teacher should read aloud from storybooks printed in *hiragana*. The students should be encouraged to read the words themselves. Textbooks in *hiragana* for young readers have spaces indicating the breaks between words, but these breaks disappear in reading materials for students who are beyond the primary level. As in English, readers first learn to pronounce the sound of the single symbols, but soon they can practice recognizing groups of symbols in common clusters.

In learning to write *hiragana*, students should give attention to the following details of orthography:

- The long *o* sound and the long *u* sound, which often convey a different meaning from the short vowel sounds, are written with an "extra" *hiragana u* う . For example, *doro* (mud) どろ and *dōro* (street) どうろ .

- A small subscript *hiragana tsu* っ is written before consonants that are heard as "double" consonants. This small *tsu* indicates the difference between *kako* (the past) かこ and *kakko* (parentheses) かっこう.

- Two dots at the upper right of syllables beginning with unvoiced consonants make the beginning consonant a voiced one. For example, *ka* か becomes *ga* が, *sa* さ becomes *za* ざ, and *ta* た becomes *da* だ .

- In the case of syllables beginning with *h*, such as *ha* は and *hi* ひ , two dots in the upper right makes them *ba* ば and *bi* び , but a small circle ゜ makes the syllables *pa* ぱ , *pi* ぴ , and so on.

- Eleven syllables that begin with a consonant and end in the *i* sound (like *ki* き , *gi* ぎ , *shi* し, and so on) take a small subscript *ya* や , *yu* ゆ , or *yo* よ to make blends *kya* きゃ , *kyu* きゅ , *kyo* きょ , and so on. The blends that end in *u* or *o*, such as *kyu* きゅ and *kyo* きょ, can be followed by another *hiragana u* う to elongate the *u* or the *o* sound: *kyu* きゅう , *kyo* きょう , and so on.

- Certain *hiragana* symbols used as grammatical particles in sentences take an irregular pronunciation: the *ha* symbol は is used for the particle *wa, he* へ for *e,* and *wo* を for *o.*

After a few weeks of practice, students can use *hiragana* to write all the words and sentences they can say. Teachers use many techniques that are familiar to California teachers—such as the language experience approach—for stimulating group and individual composition. Although writing in *hiragana* alone appears to be childlike, complete sentences and essays can be written in *hiragana*. All beginning students should learn to read and write in *hiragana*.

Katakana

After students master the fairly regular rules of *hiragana* orthography, they learn the parallel *katakana* syllabary. Because the context or origin of words determines whether they are written in *katakana,* instruction should focus on examples and principles of correct usage of *katakana*. A few conventions of orthography are different from those in *hiragana*. For example, an extended vowel sound is shown by the use of a bar —, as in *apaato* (apartment)アパート. Also, consonant + vowel sounds that do not occur in Japanese are possible in *katakana,* and foreign words can be adapted to Japanese text by the use of subscript vowels. For example, the word "film" is a problem because no Japanese syllable exists for *fi*. So the *katakana fu* is written with a small subscript *i* following, イ , to begin the word *fuirumu*フィルム (film).

Katakana workbooks also are available in the specialty bookstores. Students encounter *katakana* less frequently in storybooks, however, so instruction is usually a more protracted process, taking up new uses and features of *katakana* as they arise in reading textbooks during the first two years of reading instruction.

Kanji

Chinese characters, called *kanji,* are introduced to students in the first grade. Even before students have perfectly mastered *kana* orthography, they are introduced to simple characters. Characters first appear in reading material with their pronunciation written in small *hiragana* alongside as a clue. This small *hiragana* key is called *furigana*. Textbooks for all subjects introduce new characters for abstract concepts and historical names, with their pronunciation alongside in *furigana*. From the first grade to the ninth grade, students should focus heavily on the recognition and writing of *kanji*.

To introduce the reading lesson, the teacher reads aloud while the students follow a written passage with their eyes. The text is a unit of information or a short story. The teacher remarks on the new words in the passage and asks the students to read sentence by sentence as a group or individually. This approach is similar to the guided reading approach used in English reading lessons in the primary grades. The teacher asks questions of the students to check for comprehension. Discussion of the story sometimes moves to the motives and feelings of the characters (or the similar experiences of the students) to promote the students' engagement with the story as a whole.

The second part of the reading lesson concentrates mainly on learning to recognize and write the new characters, or *kanji,* that have appeared in the reading passage. The teacher writes the new characters on the chalkboard. The new characters may also be arranged in the student's workbook that accompanies the reader. In introducing a new character to the students, the teacher should give attention to the following points: the stroke order, *on*-readings and *kun*-readings, and *okurigana.*

The stroke-order for writing the character. The teacher faces the chalkboard, back to students, and writes the character in large, slow motions with the side of the chalk. The teacher counts each stroke out loud, because the order of writing the strokes is prescribed and the counting of strokes is important for use in learning dictionary skills later. The students first follow the teacher's strokes with large arm movements in the air; they then apply their pencils to their workbooks, counting out loud as they make each stroke. The workbook or copybook may give examples of the character faintly printed in square boxes, so the student may trace over the model several times. The students practice writing the character within the squared lines for themselves, striving for correct angles and proportions. The general rule for stroke order is to complete the strokes from top to bottom and left to right. As students gain experience, they eventually learn to guess the stroke order for most new *kanji* they encounter. The following exercise is from a Japanese writing book:

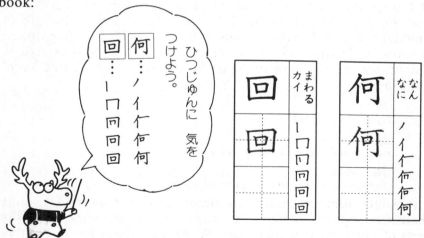

Source: *Kokugo 2-Nen Kyōkasho Pittari Tesuto.* Tokyo: Shinko Shuppansha Keirinkan, n.d., p. 18. Used by permission of the publisher.

***On-**readings and **kun-**readings of each character.* In the context of a sentence, each *kanji* usually has one proper pronunciation. When the character is abstracted from context for study, its two or more possible pronunciations are discussed by the teacher. The *on*-reading is derived from Chinese and is usually the pronunciation of the character when it appears in compounds. The *kun*-reading is the pronunciation when the character appears alone. Only *on*- and *kun*-readings that commonly are used in the oral vocabulary of the children are introduced in elementary school. Uncommon readings of the *kanji* are postponed until junior high school or later. The teacher reviews single characters out of context with the students, asking what is the *on*-reading and what is the *kun*-reading. Then the teacher presents the character in the context of phrases or sentences and asks the students to name the appropriate reading. Students learn to judge the correct reading of the character from the context. In workbook exercises and quizzes, the students write in *hiragana* the proper reading of characters in a sentence or, conversely, write the correct characters for words presented in *hiragana* in the sentence.

火

Kun-reading ひ (*hi*)
When used alone as "fire"

火山

On-reading か (*ka*)
When used in compounds
kazan = volcano

Okurigana. The earliest characters introduced at the beginning of first grade are nouns used alone or in compound nouns that do not take any grammatical ending. When a *kanji* is used as the root of a modifier or verb, however, it must take a grammatical ending written in *hiragana*. The *hiragana* that completes the word is called *okurigana*. The proper use of *okurigana* must be learned with each new *kanji*. For example:

tsuyo i = strong (adjective)

tsuyo maru = grow strong (intransitive verb)

強 める
tsuyo meru = make strong (transitive verb)

Although some characters are simply two or three strokes, most characters appear more complicated, as if they are made up of the parts of other, simpler characters. When a character has discernibly different components, some portion of the character is taken as the radical, the component part by which the character will be arranged in dictionaries and card catalogs. About 200 radicals make up the categories by which *kanji* are analyzed and grouped. Teachers introduce the name of the radical as part of the introduction of each new *kanji*. Each radical is derived from a basic character and is identified by the meaning of that basic character. For example, the character for mouth alone is a square box, pronounced *kuchi*, which becomes the *kuchi* radical *(kuchi-hen)* when seen at the left of other characters. Some of the characters that have a *kuchi* radical convey something to do with the mouth.

口	叱	味	咲く
kuchi	*shikaru*	*aji*	*saku*
mouth	scold	flavor	bloom

These three characters have a *kuchi* radical.

Reading and Writing Exercises

After practice in reading and writing the new characters in the textbook, students build their vocabulary and grammar skills. Students learn synonyms and antonyms, the transformation of adjectives into nouns, and similar grammatical points. Students practice these points by constructing or correcting sample sentences in their workbooks.

Beyond textbook and workbook-type writing practice, students are taught to organize information and feelings into *sakubun* (compositions). Very young students may simply write messages to the teacher beginning with the salutation *Sensei ano ne* (Teacher, I want to tell you . . .). The teacher writes a simple reply on the page and returns it to the student. Students may be asked to write about an event in which the whole class participated, to write an ending to an unfinished story, or to keep a diary. Students usually use newsprint copybooks that have been squared with blue or black lines for composition. The squares become smaller as the students advance through the grades. From the upper elementary or junior high school years, students use paper that is squared into 200 or 400 squares, called *genkō yoshi*. This manuscript-writing paper is used by adults as well for drafting compositions or documents. *Genkō yoshi* is available in stores that sell Japanese stationery supplies.

The standard reading instructional textbooks used in Japanese public schools are not commercially available, but the California school might acquire such textbooks through the Japanese Ministry of Education-sponsored *Nihonjin Gakkō* Saturday schools in Los Angeles or San Francisco. Several publishers in Japan issue series

68

of readers and workbooks that parallel the national curricula and that are designed for use at home (*juku*). These privately published reading and practice books are in themselves quite a complete set of materials and are available in specialty bookstores in California. Such materials, however, assume that one has much knowledge about life in Japan. On the other hand, some of the materials are intended for nonnative speakers of Japanese. Introductions and explanations in such textbooks and workbooks are in English, an approach which may or may not be appropriate for teachers and students in a particular California school.

Another reality of teaching Japanese language development in California must also be anticipated. Instructional staff who can compare teaching methods in Japan and California soon realize that in Japan every school lesson is a language and reading lesson. In social studies, science, mathematics, art, music, and sports, students are constantly building new vocabulary, *kanji* recognition, and expressive skills in Japanese. Thus, the teachers in Japan can assume a great degree of support for Japanese reading in the total school environment of the students. The California school's Japanese language teachers cannot usually make such an assumption. Teachers of Japanese in California schools are likely to feel the pressure of teaching vocabulary from many fields to the students—mathematical expressions, science concepts, geography, and history—so as to build the entire stock of academic language skills that are common to educated native speakers of Japanese. This tension is not peculiar to Japanese; all dual language development efforts everywhere face the same dilemma. However, the teaching of reading and writing to Japanese speakers in California schools must not proceed only on the basis of given materials or in direct replication of language education in Japan. Teachers of language development in California will need to consider methods in conjunction with the special constraints and special goals acknowledged in the local setting. For the suggested content for teaching reading and writing in Japan, see Appendix C.

Methods for Teaching Writing in Japanese

The bamboo brush (*fude*) and black charcoal ink (*sumi*) are used for writing formal personal correspondence, official notices or certificates, and decorative calligraphy. Training in brush writing is not essential in order to read and write Japanese, but it is a part of the literacy education of most Japanese native speakers. Students can learn to use a brush and ink once they are well coordinated in writing with a pencil. Practice in brush writing helps to improve handwriting with a pen or pencil, because the prescribed shapes of stroke endings (such as a tapered ending or a hooked ending) are very clear when written with a brush.

When students have learned how to hold the brush, they practice basic vertical and horizontal strokes. Each student needs brushes, *sumi* ink, a slate ink dish called a *tsuzuri,* water, and paper. Newsprint or even torn up newspapers can be used for practice paper; a special white paper for calligraphy is best for final work. Beginners write simple Chinese characters alone in large format on the page. Often these characters have a positive meaning. More advanced students make characters in smaller scale and begin to copy "samplers" from classical literature. Special styles of *hiragana* also are written with the brush. The teacher traditionally uses red ink to make corrections on the student's work or to draw a circle around work that is well executed.

When the brushes and ink appear in a bilingual classroom, all students are likely to take an interest in trying their hand. Brush writing can easily become an activity in which the Japanese-speaking student and teacher become the models for the whole class. This is an opportunity for all to learn a little about the Japanese written language and about the art form of Japanese calligraphy. With practice, even non-Japanese speakers can learn to write a few characters with a brush. Examples of the students' best work can be hung in the classroom or exhibited at a school fair or open house (see figures 2 and 3).

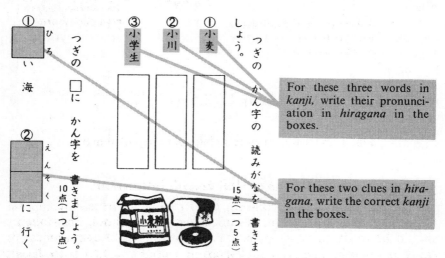

For these three words in *kanji*, write their pronunciation in *hiragana* in the boxes.

For these two clues in *hiragana*, write the correct *kanji* in the boxes.

Source: *Kokugo 2-Nen Kyōkasho Pittari Tesuto.* Tokyo: Shinko Shuppansha Keirinkan, n.d., p. 49. Used by permission of the publisher.

Fig. 2. Workbook exercises in writing *hiragana* and *kanji*

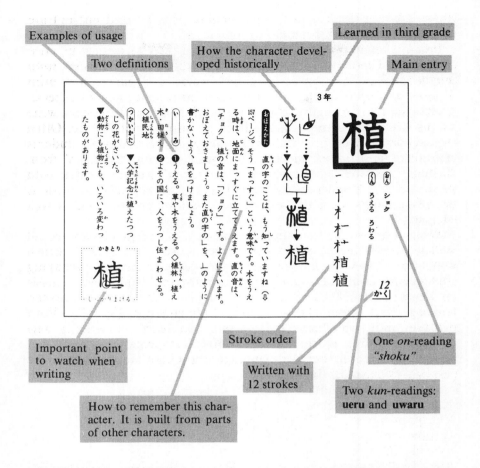

Examples of usage

Two definitions

How the character developed historically

Learned in third grade

Main entry

Important point to watch when writing

How to remember this character. It is built from parts of other characters.

Stroke order

Written with 12 strokes

One *on*-reading "*shoku*"

Two *kun*-readings: **ueru** and **uwaru**

Source: Tōdō Akiyasu and others, *Shōgakusei no Kanji Hakasei (Ichi-ni-san-nenyō)*. Tokyo: Gakutōsha, 1985, p. 158. Used by permission of the publisher.

Fig. 3. A typical entry in a children's *kanji* dictionary

Introduction of Oral English Instruction

Most limited-English-proficient (LEP) students benefit from oral English language instruction as soon as they enter school. The students should be ready to develop their basic interpersonal communicative skills in English. The critical element in school contexts is to design instructional programs for LEP students so that exposure to English results in the efficient acquisition of basic competence in communication without interference with normal cognitive or academic subject matter development. Instructional environments vary in the degree to which they promote or inhibit this process among language minority students.

In school situations language minority students are exposed to English in four basic ways: (1) submersion classes; (2) grammar-based English as a second language (ESL); (3) communication-based ESL; and (4) sheltered-English classes (see the Glossary). In submersion classes teachers instruct as if all of the students in the class were native speakers of English. Grammar-based ESL classes focus on phonology and syntax and emphasize the learning of language rules through inductive (grammar-translation) or deductive (audiolingual or cognitive code) methods. Communication-based ESL, by contrast, places emphasis on language use and language functions. This type of instruction focuses on basic communicative competence, not on the learning of rules of grammar. Sheltered-English approaches deliver subject matter in the second language. In these situations second-language acquirers usually are grouped together, special materials are provided, and students are allowed to speak in their primary language. However, the teacher always models English-native-speaker or near-native-speaker speech. Also, a native speaker-to-nonnative speaker register ("motherese" or "foreigner talk") is used by the teacher. The research suggests that communication-based ESL and sheltered-English instruction effectively promote the acquisition of basic interpersonal communicative skills in English. Grammar-based ESL and submersion classes have been found to be less effective in promoting such skills (Krashen, 1981; Terrell, 1981).

Grammar-based ESL instruction at best leads mostly to the development of the language monitor (Krashen, 1981). The monitor assists learners of English in the production of grammatically accurate utterances. However, several conditions must exist before individuals can efficiently use the monitor. First, the task must be focused on language forms in some way (for example, a grammar test). Second, the student previously must have learned the desired rule and must be able to recognize the appropriateness of the specific rule for the specific structure desired. Finally, the speaker needs sufficient time to retrieve the rule, adapt it to the speech situation, and use it correctly in producing the utterance. These conditions are not available to individuals in most normal speech situations.

Submersion Environments

Submersion environments are even less effective than grammar-based ESL, because during submersion lessons language minority students do not comprehend much of what is said. Stephen Krashen states that the critical element of "comprehensible input" is $i + 1$.

The *i* is what the student can already comprehend in the second language. The + *l* is the additional input made comprehensible by a variety of strategies and techniques (Krashen, 1981). In submersion classes, however, the provision of *i* + *l* is only infrequently achieved. Because most of the input is directed toward native English speakers, the language minority students are exposed to English input at incomprehensible levels of *i* + *2*, *i* + *3*, and *i* + *n*. Considerable research indicates that submersion does not effectively promote either the development of basic interpersonal communicative skills or cognitive/academic language proficiency among language minority students (Cummins, 1981; Krashen, 1981).

According to some recent second-language acquisition studies (Krashen, 1981; Terrell, 1981), the attainment of basic interpersonal communicative skills in a second language is largely determined by the amount of "comprehensible second-language" input a student receives under favorable conditions. Communication-based ESL and sheltered-English situations provide students with large amounts of such input under optimal conditions. Submersion environments and grammar-based ESL situations provide students with only limited amounts of "comprehensible input" (especially in the initial stages) under conditions considerably less favorable for second-language acquisition.

Unless there are important psychoeducational reasons, such as recent traumatic experiences or special learning disabilities, Japanese-speaking students will benefit from exposure to English in communication-based ESL and sheltered-English situations. Students will thereby acquire English and will not necessarily experience interference with normal cognitive or academic development or primary language development if the program also provides adequate instruction in these areas.

On the other hand, grammar-based ESL and submersion environments may work against English acquisition. First, young children and older children who have not experienced normal cognitive or academic development probably do not have cognitive processes developed well enough to assimilate the complex and decontextualized language that characterizes grammar-based ESL and submersion classes. Additionally, in some cases so much attention is placed on speaking only in grammatically correct utterances that students become inhibited in the process of acquiring a second language.

In summary, a substantial amount of research evidence suggests that submersion environments and grammar-based ESL (audiolingual, cognitive code, and grammar translation) should not be provided to language minority students until they attain sufficient levels of basic interpersonal communicative skills and cognitive or academic language proficiency to benefit from such instructional contexts. Communication-based ESL (for example, the natural approach) and sheltered-English classes are effective in promoting the development of basic interpersonal communicative skills in English for students at any age and at any developmental or academic level.

Reading in Two Languages

There are basically four choices in organizing a reading program in bilingual contexts. Classical bilingual education programs usually begin literacy instruction in Japanese and then, at a determined stage, introduce English language reading instruction. Some compensatory bilingual programs provide simultaneous instruction in both Japanese and English. Immersion programs are organized to initiate literacy in a second language and then to introduce the students' first language. Finally, in ESL-only programs, literacy instruction is provided only in English. In this section each of these approaches will be described and evaluated in terms of possible outcomes for most Japanese-speaking students.

Using Japanese Followed by English

When sufficient human and material resources are available and parental support is present, the first-language reading approach has proved to be effective (Cummins, 1981). In the most successful programs students are given full first-language literacy instruction in kindergarten and grades one through three. At approximately the third-grade level, if a student has made normal reading progress, formal English reading is introduced. Reading instruction in the students' first language is continued until at least the sixth-grade level (Rosier and Holm, 1980; Cummins, 1981). This practice is critical because the effects of reading instruction are cumulative, showing the best results after five to seven years (Cummins, 1981). Many studies indicate that proficient bilingual and biliterate students have definite advantages over other language minority students and even over monolingual majority students (Cummins, 1981; Kessler and Quinn, 1980; *Evaluation of California's Education Services,* 1981).

Using Japanese and English Simultaneously

In some bilingual programs reading instruction in Japanese and English is presented to limited- and non-English-speaking students simultaneously. This may be a particularly attractive option for Japanese-English bilingual programs where the student could learn a logographic and alphabetic system at the same time. Cognitive confusion (for example, false cognates) that has been alleged between two alphabetic systems would not present a problem in a Japanese-

English program. The students would be learning to associate two totally different symbolic systems (English and Japanese) with a common set of concepts (description, action, and so forth).

The key to an effective, simultaneous literacy program is coordination of the reading activities in the two languages. In light of the notion of the common underlying proficiency (Cummins, 1981), it is not necessary to teach the same or equivalent skills in both languages. It would be much more efficient to choose activities that were appropriate to the student's reading level, emphasizing different skills in each language, depending on the content and the student's needs. If different teachers are responsible for the two literacy activities, it is essential that they plan and coordinate their work carefully. If one teacher handles both languages, it is advisable that the two languages be separated in terms of time, materials, and environment. Simultaneous literacy instruction does not mean mixing languages in the same activity. Rather, it should involve complementing and enhancing the student's literacy development through the use of two languages in separate, efficient, challenging sets of activities.

Using English Followed by Japanese

Immersion programs in French for native English-speaking students have been in operation in Canada for more than a decade. Several experimental immersion programs also have been conducted in the United States. In such programs all initial instruction, including literacy, is given through the students' second language. In the second or third grade, English–language arts are added to the curriculum. An enormous amount of research has shown that most students in French immersion programs achieve high levels of literacy in both languages (Cummins, 1981; Krashen, 1981; Genesee, 1980; *Studies on Immersion Education,* 1984). Even though students were provided with most of their instruction in French, once English language arts were added to the curriculum, the students quickly caught up to their monolingually schooled peers. In fact, the students in the immersion program did as well in English reading as did the students in English-only programs (Genesee, 1980). In addition, of course, the students had the added benefit of French proficiency.

One should note that the immersion programs are especially designed so that native English-speaking students acquire a second language while at the same time experiencing normal academic and English development. These students, in general, attain a level of proficient bilingualism. Implementing such programs for minority students in the U.S. should be based on a commitment by educators to promote the LEP students' academic learning as well as comparable proficiency in both English and their native language.

Using English Only

For a variety of reasons—philosophical position, desires of some students and parents, or lack of educational resources—some school districts continue to provide Japanese-speaking students with English-only, submersion-type reading instruction. Fortunately, most programs provide at least oral ESL instruction; nevertheless, few recognized ESL (initial) literacy curricula are available; and few staff members are trained in this approach. Unfortunately, most of the activities in the ESL program tend to be remedial versions of the same activities used with native speakers of English. The failure of submersion and ESL-only programs is well documented in the literature (Cummins, 1981; Krashen, 1981).

Under the best circumstances within the English-only option, formal English reading instruction should be delayed until language minority students have acquired some basic interpersonal communicative skills in English. Once an oral language base in English is established, students will be better able to assimilate the more cognitively demanding concepts associated with literacy. Educators should be aware, however, that since Japanese instruction is not addressed, a subtractive form of bilingualism probably will result for most students.

Clearly, English-only reading instruction is not a recommended option. However, should resources not be available or should parents decline a Japanese language approach, then the only alternative may be an instructional program conducted entirely in English. Under these circumstances the following suggestions are given:

1. Provide students with ample amounts of "comprehensible second-language input" in English for the acquisition of basic interpersonal communicative skills.
2. Provide cognitive/academic language development through sheltered-English strategies.
3. Group second-language acquirers apart from native speakers for some oral language and initial literacy instruction in English so that they may benefit from communication-based ESL and sheltered-English strategies.
4. Sequence instruction appropriately so that students will not be introduced to new concepts until they have acquired the appropriate linguistic and academic background sufficient to assimilate more complex skills.
5. Analyze English reading materials in order to anticipate where the students may have difficulties with vocabulary, syntax, and cultural content. Provide the students with supplemental instruction so that these difficulties can be overcome.
6. Provide interested parents with materials and instructions to carry out language tasks at home in Japanese. Teachers should

encourage these parents to focus on those tasks that will better prepare their children for the academic requirements of school.

7. Teach students study skills that will help them analyze unfamiliar materials, research unknown concepts, use library resources, and so forth.

Summarizing the Discussion on Strategies

Historically, parents and educators have considered the acquisition of basic interpersonal communicative skills in English as the only critical need for language minority students. While these skills are very important, the development of cognitive/academic language proficiency seems to be even more critical to school success. One way cognitive/academic language proficiency can be developed is through Japanese. Opportunities to develop cognitive/academic language skills in Japanese are not commonly available to students in most communities in California. Therefore, parents and educators must work together to design and implement such activities in the home, school, and community. On the other hand, opportunities to develop basic interpersonal communicative skills in English are naturally present in some language minority homes, most communities, and all schools. Those cognitive/academic language skills not learned in Japanese can be added easily in English by specially designed instruction at school.

If students are to benefit from their bilingualism, attention to Japanese language development and English language acquisition is necessary. Without this attention, many Japanese-speaking children will continue to have serious language, academic, and cultural problems at school. The task of educating language minority students is not simple. Nevertheless, recently, creative and committed educators in tandem with concerned parents have designed and implemented, for language minority students, educational programs that have resulted in (1) high levels of English language proficiency; (2) normal cognitive/academic development; (3) positive adjustment to both the minority and majority cultures; and (4) high levels of Japanese language development. The purpose of this handbook has been to assist school personnel, parents, and community members in achieving similar goals.

Glossary

Additive bilingualism. A process by which individuals develop proficiency in a second language subsequent to or simultaneously with the development of proficiency in the primary language.

Affective filter. A construct developed to refer to the screening effects of personality, motivation, and other feelings on second language learning. The filter is "high" when the learner is tense, uncomfortable, or defensive, but "low" when the learner is comfortable and receptive. Whether the affective filter is high or low affects each learner's absorption or processing of "comprehensible input" (Krashen, 1981).

Agglutination. A feature of some languages, such as Japanese and Turkish, in which compound words or whole phrases are built by stringing together simple root words that do not change their form or meaning. Agglutinative languages are contrasted with inflectional languages, such as English, in which meaning is altered by spelling changes within words.

Basic interpersonal communicative skills (BICS). Language skills at the level of ordinary conversational fluency of most native speakers. These skills usually are not taught or learned at school, but in the home or community. Since basic interpersonal communicative skills are the common ground of all native speakers of any language, they are necessary but not sufficient for success in reading and academic subjects. James Cummins first used this term, but he subsequently refined the notion in terms of "cognitively undemanding contextualized" language. Cummins contrasts this level of language with "cognitive/academic language proficiency" (Cummins, 1981).

Bilingual education program. In reference to Japanese bilingual education, an organized curriculum that includes Japanese language development, English language learning, and school subject-area learning through both Japanese and English. The Japanese bilingual education program has one goal in addition to the regular goals of the school curriculum; this goal is that the participating students will develop proficient bilingualism.

Chinese character. Logographs adopted from the Chinese written language into the Japanese written language. The Japanese term *kanji* literally means Chinese character. A character stands for a given word, or sometimes for two or more words, so its meaning can be ascertained only from the context. The pronunciation of a Chinese character is not conveyed by its form. About 3,000 Chinese characters are used in modern Japanese; in addition, many compounds are made from two or more characters.

Cognitive/academic language proficiency (CALP). A level of language skills strongly associated with literacy and academic achievement. James Cummins first used this term, but he later refined the notion to that of "cognitively demanding decontextualized" language (1981). This proficiency involves a greater vocabulary, more complicated syntax, and a higher level of abstraction than do "basic interpersonal communicative skills" (Cummins, 1981).

Communication-based English as a second language. A second-language instructional approach in which the goals, teaching methods, and assessments of students' progress are all based on behavioral objectives defined in terms of abilities to communicate messages in English. In communication-based ESL, the focus is on language function and use and not on formal grammar. Examples of communication-based ESL instructional approaches include "Suggestopedia," natural approach, and community language learning (Terrell, 1981).

Comprehensible second-language input. A term used by Stephen Krashen to denote lessons or lectures in the second language that are carefully planned to build on the second-language comprehension level the students have already attained. If the students already know a degree of English (i), the lesson or all lessons in a given period should use these skills plus a range of new words and structures (i + 1). Strategies include (1) a focus on communicative content rather than on language forms per se; (2) frequent use of concrete contextual referents; (3) lack of restrictions on the students' use of their first language during lessons, especially in the early stages; (4) careful grouping practices; (5) minimal overt language form correction by teachers; and (6) stimulating and motivating experiences.

Eigo. The Japanese term meaning "the English language."

Fude. A bamboo brush with bristles made of horsehair. It is used for traditional calligraphy arts and formal or ceremonial writings.

Furigana. Small *kana* running alongside *kanji* in a text to simplify the reading of the Chinese characters. *Furigana* usually is written in *hiragana*. Anyone with a knowledge of *hiragana* can then pronounce unknown characters.

Gakkō. The Japanese word for "school." Japanese language schools are called *Nihongo Gakkō.* Japanese Saturday schools for students who want to keep up with the educational curricula in Japan are called *Nihonjin Gakkō,* or Japanese people's schools.

Genkō yoshi. Manuscript paper used for writing school essays and assignments in Japanese. The paper is lined both horizontally and vertically into a pattern of boxes. Students use this paper when they are learning to write *kanji* and *kana* of equal size and with even spacing.

Grammar-based English as a second language. An ESL approach in which the goals, teaching methods, and student evaluations are all based on behavioral objectives related to the students' production of grammatically correct sentences in English. The focus is on language form and usage, not on language function and use. Examples of grammar-based ESL approaches include grammar-translation, audiolingualism, and cognitive code (Terrell, 1981).

Hiragana. A phonemic syllabary, in which each "letter" represents a syllable. *Hiragana* usually is the first writing system learned by Japanese students. There are 48 basic *hiragana* symbols, plus several archaic ones found in old literature. Special superscript marks are used to modify some *hiragana* to change initial consonant sounds.

Immersion program. An organized second-language learning curriculum for students who speak the majority language (English) as their native language. In addition to the regular goals of the school, the immersion program's one extra goal is proficient bilingualism for participating students. The curriculum includes native language development, second language learning, and subject-area learning through the second language (*Studies on Immersion Education,* 1984).

Issei. In Japanese, literally, the "first generation," referring to Japanese-born persons who immigrated to Hawaii, North America, or South America. The American-born children of *issei* are *nisei.*

Japanese. Refers to the language, the people, and the products of the country of Japan.

Japanese-American. Used to describe Americans of Japanese ancestry. The term is used to denote the community or traditions of Japanese-American people as distinguished from those of either Japanese or other ethnic American people.

Juku. A school that operates after normal school hours and on weekends in Japan. Students usually enroll in a *juku* to strengthen skills learned in public school and to practice test-taking skills that they need to pass high school or university entrance examinations.

Kana. The generic term for either or both of the phonemic syllabaries in the Japanese writing system, *hiragana* and *katakana.*

Kana-zukai. Literally, "the use of *kana.*" Refers to the way that *kanji* and *kana* are combined in words or sentences and to the correct combinations of *kana* that represent certain sounds and blends. The objectives for primary-level Japanese language teaching include a concern for students' correct *kana-zukai.*

Kanji. The Japanese term for the "Chinese characters" that are used in written Japanese.

Katakana. One of two syllabaries in written Japanese, in which each symbol stands for a syllable. *Katakana* is often used to transliterate foreign words and names into Japanese, and it is used for the full text of domestic telegrams. Some *katakana* visually resemble their counterpart *hiragana,* though some do not, in the way that some capital letters in the English alphabet resemble small letters, but some do not. *Katakana* is never mixed with *hiragana* in the same word.

Katei kyōshi. The Japanese term for a "home tutor." This is typically a university student hired by a family to drill a child in language or mathematics lessons in order to reinforce the school curriculum.

Kenjinkai. An association (*kai*) of people (*jin*) from the same geographical prefecture (*ken*) of Japan. Even in Tokyo there are associations of people from the same rural prefectures. They get together for social and mutual assistance purposes, and the custom continues in the cities of California to some extent.

Kokugo. Literally, "national language," meaning Japanese. A required subject in the curriculum through grade eleven. Just as in the American subject of "English," the *kokugo* curriculum covers basic literacy, grammar, functional uses of language, literary appreciation, and creative writing.

Kun-reading or *kun-yomi*. The "Japanese" pronunciation of a Chinese character, usually appropriate when the character is used alone as a single word. The *kun*-reading contrasts with the *on*-reading in compounds. Students must learn from practice and exposure which pronunciation of a character is correct in which context.

Kyōiku. Literally, "education." This word appears in many compounds such as *kyōiku mama*, a mother who pushes her child's school achievement, or *kyōiku kanji*, the basic set of Chinese characters children learn in elementary school.

Limited bilingualism. A level of bilingualism at which an individual cannot be considered an educated native speaker of either the first or second language. Although a person may have basic interpersonal communicative skills in Japanese and English, neither language has been developed to include the cognitive/academic language proficiency.

Meiji. Refers to the Meiji Emperor or the period of his reign, 1868 to 1912.

Monitor. A construct developed to refer to the mental mechanism by which learners process, store, and retrieve conscious rules of language. Conscious rules are placed in the monitor as one learns a second language and come to bear on the language produced by the learner. To effectively use the monitor, language learners must (1) have sufficient time to retrieve the desired rule; (2) be involved in a task focused on language forms and not on language functions; and (3) have previously learned correctly and stored the rule. These three conditions rarely are present in normal conversational situations (Krashen, 1981).

Nihon or nippon. Japanese terms for the country of Japan.

Nihongo. The Japanese term for "the Japanese language."

Nihonjin. Japanese term for "Japanese person" or "Japanese people."

Nikkeijin. A term from the Japanese language meaning Japanese-American person or persons.

Nisei. A Japanese term meaning "second generation," referring to Americans born of *issei* Japanese immigrant parents.

Okurigana. The *hiragana* ending to a word whose root is expressed in writing with a Chinese character.

On-reading or on-yomi. The "Chinese pronunciation" of Chinese characters borrowed from the Chinese written language. These readings are not necessarily akin to Chinese pronunciations of the same characters today, but they contrast with *kun*-readings, based on older, indigenous Japanese words. The *on*-reading of a character is often its reading in compounds. Many characters have more than one *on*-reading, so practice is necessary to learn how a character is read in particular compounds.

Partial bilingualism. A level of bilingualism at which individuals attain native-like proficiency in one language but lesser skills in the second language. In the case of Japanese and English, a partially bilingual person has a full range of understanding, speaking, reading, and writing skills in one of the two languages but not in both. For instance, such an individual might read but not speak English or speak but not read Japanese.

Proficient bilingualism. A level of bilingualism at which individuals attain native-like proficiency in two languages. Proficient bilingualism in Japanese and English means mastery of understanding, speaking, reading, and writing skills in both languages.

Radical. A portion of the written Chinese character by which it is grouped with other characters sharing the same radical for ordering in character dictionaries, the library card catalog, the telephone directory, and so on.

Romaji. The Japanese term for the Roman alphabet.

Sakubun. "Creative composition" in Japanese. This is a standard exercise for writing practice in the language development curriculum in Japanese schools.

Sansei. A term derived from Japanese meaning "third generation," describing persons born in the Japanese-American community whose grandparents were *Issei.*

Sensei. The Japanese term for "teacher." The community priest, doctor, and even senior legislators or other respected leaders are also called *sensei.* When attached to the teacher's name, the term comes last, as in Miyazaki-sensei or Suzuki-sensei.

Sheltered-English classes. Subject-matter class periods taught in English to students who are still learning English as a second language. In this approach teachers (1) group students of the same English level; (2) speak in a native speaker-to-nonnative speaker register similar to "motherese" or "foreigner talk"; and (3) proceed from the student's present level of skill in English and the subject area to gradually higher levels, using substantial amounts of "comprehensible second-language input" (Krashen, 1981).

Shōsha. The Japanese term for "company" or "business." The group of Japanese nationals living in California in connection with jobs in trading or manufacturing firms is often called the *Shōsha* community.

Shōwa. The era of the present emperor of Japan, whose reign began in 1926. The *Shōwa* dating system is more commonly used in Japan than is the Western year. The year 1926 was the first year of *Shōwa,* so *Shōwa* 61 refers to 1986. To convert the *Shōwa* year to the Western calendar year, add 25.

Shūji. The Japanese art of calligraphy with a bamboo brush.

Submersion classes. Subject-matter class periods taught in English to mixed groups of native speakers of English and students still learning English as a second language. Teachers in such classes speak in a native speaker-to-native speaker register and provide only minimal amounts of "comprehensible second-language input" (Krashen, 1981).

Submersion program. An organized curriculum designed for native speakers of a language but often used with limited-English-proficient students. No special instructional activities focus on the needs of the LEP students. Rather, these students are grouped together with native speakers to "sink or swim." In such programs LEP students commonly experience a form of subtractive bilingualism, usually limited bilingualism.

Subtractive bilingualism. The interruption of the development of language skills in the first language or the loss of those skills because of the disuse or suppression of the first language in the school program. In the case of Japanese and English, a school program that neither encourages nor teaches the development of Japanese speaking, reading, and writing skills, but that emphasizes only English, is likely to result in subtractive bilingualism.

Sumi. Black charcoal ink used for calligraphy.

Transitional bilingual education program. An organized curriculum that uses the first language of LEP students for some period of time after the students enter the school or district. For Japanese-speaking LEP students, such a program would include (1) Japanese language development; (2) English-as-a-second-language classes; and (3) school subjects taught through both Japanese and English. In an "early" transitional bilingual program, a student would be removed from Japanese language activities as soon as he or she achieved basic interpersonal communicative skills. The student then would be placed in an English-only submersion program. In a "late" transitional program, the LEP Japanese speaker would continue to receive Japanese language development and Japanese assistance in subject areas until cognitive/academic language proficiency in English is achieved.

Tsuzuri. A slate ink-stone with a depression that holds the liquid ink for brush-writing.

Yonsei. A fourth-generation Japanese American.

Bibliography

Selected References

Ada, Alma Flor. "No One Learns to Read Twice: The Transferability of Reading Skills," *Aids to Bilingual Communication Report,* Vol. 6 (January, 1980).

Anderson, Ronald S. *Education in Japan, a Century of Modern Development* (107-080-01339-8). Washington, D.C.: U.S. Government Printing Office, 1975.

Asahi Evening News (Tokyo), April 9, 1986. "4.5 million students attended *juku* in 1985."

Bailey, Nathalie, and others. "Is There a 'Natural Sequence' in Adult Second Language Learning?" *Language Learning,* Vol. 24 (December, 1974), 235—43.

Chuman, Frank F. *The Bamboo People: The Law and Japanese-Americans.* Los Angeles: Japanese American Citizens League, 1976.

Conroy, Francis H. *The Japanese Expansion into Hawaii, 1868—1898.* San Francisco: Research Associates, 1973.

Course of Study for Elementary Schools in Japan, Notification No. 155. Tokyo: Ministry of Education, Science and Culture, Educational and Cultural Exchange Division, 1983.

Course of Study for Lower Secondary Schools in Japan, Notification No. 156. Tokyo: Ministry of Education, Science and Culture, Educational and Cultural Exchange Division, 1983.

Cummings, William K. *Education and Equality in Japan.* Princeton, N.J.: Princeton University Press, 1980.

Cummins, J. "The Role of Primary Language Development in Promoting Educational Success for Language Minority Students," in *Schooling and Language Minority Students: A Theoretical Framework.* Developed by the California State Department of Education; Office of Bilingual Bicultural Education. Los Angeles: Evaluation, Dissemination and Assessment Center, California State University, Los Angeles, 1981.

Daniels, Roger. *The Politics of Prejudice: The Anti-Japanese Movement in California and the Struggle for Japanese Exclusion.* New York: Atheneum Publications, 1968.

Dulay, Heidi C., and Marina Burt. "Natural Sequences in Child Second Language Acquisition," *Language Learning,* Vol. 24 (June, 1974), 37—53.

Education in Japan: A Graphic Presentation. Tokyo: Ministry of Education, Science and Culture, Research and Statistics Division, 1982.

Evaluation of California's Educational Services to Limited- and Non-English-Speaking Students, Final Report. San Francisco: Development Associates, Inc. 1981.

The Experience of Japanese Americans in the United States: A Teacher's Resource Manual. San Francisco: Japanese American Citizens League, Ethnic Heritage Advisory Council, 1974.

Facts About Japan: Education in Japan. Tokyo: Ministry of Foreign Affairs, 1979.

Facts and Figures of Japan. Tokyo: Foreign Press Center, 1980.

Fathman, Ann. "The Relationship Between Age and Second Language Productive Ability," *Language Learning,* Vol. 25 (December, 1975), 245—53.

Genesee, F. "Acquisition of Reading Skills in Immersion Programs," *Foreign Language Annals* (February, 1980).

Gillis, Mary, and Rose Marie Weber. "The Emergence of Sentence Modalities in the English of Japanese-Speaking Children," *Language Learning,* Vol. 26 (June, 1976), 77—94.

Hachiya, Noriko. "A Comparative Study on the Value Differences of the Japanese Students and the American Students." English abstract in *Patterns of Communication In and Out of Japan.* Edited by Mayumi Hara. Tokyo: International Christian University, 1974.

Hakuta, Kenji. "A Case Study of a Japanese Child Learning English as a Second Language," *Language Learning,* Vol. 26 (December, 1976), 321—51.

Herman, Masako. *The Japanese in America, 1843—1973.* A Chronology and Factbook. Ethnic Chronology Series, No. 15. Dobbs Ferry, N.Y.: Oceana Publications, Inc. 1974.

Hosokawa, Bill. *Nisei: The Quiet Americans.* New York: William Morrow & Co., Inc., 1969.

Ichihashi, Yamato. *Japanese in the United States: A Critical Study of the Problems of the Japanese Immigrants and Their Children.* American Immigration Collection Series, No. 1. Salem, N.H.: Ayer Company Publications, Inc., 1969.

Jansen, Maurius B. "Changing Japanese Attitudes Toward Modernization," in *Changing Japanese Attitudes Toward Modernization.* Edited by Maurius B. Jansen. Rutland, Vt.: Charles E. Tuttle Co., Inc., 1982.

The Japanese Experience in America: Immigration. Supplement for U.S. History and Civics. San Francisco: San Francisco Unified School District, 1971.

Kanazawa, S. *The Common Origin of the Japanese and Korean Languages.* Tokyo: Sanseido, 1910.

Kessler, C., and M. Quinn, "Bilingualism and Science Problem-Solving Ability," *Bilingual Education Paper Series,* Vol. 4, No. 1 (August, 1980). Los Angeles: National Dissemination and Assessment Center, California State University, Los Angeles.

Kitano, Harry H. *Japanese Americans: The Evolution of a Subculture* (Second edition). Ethnic Groups in American Life Series. Englewood Cliffs, N.J.: Prentice-Hall, Inc., 1976.

Krashen, S. "Bilingual Education and Second Language Acquisition Theory," in *Schooling and Language Minority Students: A Theoretical Framework.* Developed by the California State Department of Education,

Office of Bilingual Bicultural Education. Los Angeles: Evaluation, Dissemination and Assessment Center, California State University, Los Angeles, 1981.

Lakoff, Robin T. *Language and Woman's Place.* New York: Harper and Row Publications, Inc., 1975.

Lambert, W. "Additive Versus Subtractive Forms of Bilingualism: Confusions Regarding Programs of Immersion." Paper presented at the Second Annual Language Assessment Institute, National College of Education, Chicago, June, 1982.

McDowell, Edwin. "The Japanese in Brazil," *Americas,* Vol. 32 (April, 1980), 33—39.

Miller, Roy A. *The Japanese Language.* Chicago: University of Chicago Press, 1980.

Miller, Roy A. *Japanese and Other Altaic Languages.* History and Structure of Language Series. Chicago: University of Chicago Press, 1971.

Miller, Roy A. *Origins of the Japanese Language.* Publications on Asia of the School for International Studies, No. 34. Seattle: University of Washington Press, 1981.

Millis, Harry Alvin. *The Japanese Problem in the United States.* Asian Experience in North America Series. Edited by Roger Daniels. Salem, N.H.: Ayer Company Publications, Inc., 1979.

Nelson, Andrew N. *The Modern Reader's Japanese-English Character Dictionary.* Tokyo: Charles E. Tuttle Co., Inc., 1973.

Okamoto-Bichard, Fumiko. "Mother Tongue Maintenance and Second-Language Learning: A Case of Japanese Children," *Language Learning,* Vol. 35 (March, 1985), 63—89.

Ono, Susumu. *The Origin of the Japanese Language.* Japan Life and Culture Series. San Francisco: Japan Publications Training Center, 1970.

Race of the Population by State (PC80-51-3). Washington, D.C.: U.S. Department of Commerce, Bureau of the Census, 1980.

Reischauer, Edwin O. *Japan: The Story of a Nation* (Revised edition). New York: Alfred A. Knopf, Inc., 1974.

Rosier, P., and W. Holm. "The Rock Point Experience: A Longitudinal Study of a Navajo School (Saad Naaki Bee N'nitin)," *Bilingual Education Series,* No. 8. Arlington. Va.: Center for Applied Linguistics, 1980.

Schooling and Language Minority Students: A Theoretical Framework. Prepared by the California State Department of Education. Los Angeles: California State University, Los Angeles, 1981.

Statistics on Numbers of Japanese Citizens Living Overseas (Kaigai Zairyū Hōjinsū Chōsa Tokei). Tokyo: Ministry of Foreign Affairs, 1986.

Status of Education of Children Overseas (Kaigai Shijo Kyōiku no Genjō). Tokyo: Ministry of Education, Science and Culture, Office of Overseas Children's Education, 1986.

Steinberg, Danny D., and Jun Yamada. "Are Whole Word Kanji Easier to Learn Than Syllable Kana?" *Reading Research Quarterly,* Vol. 14, No. 1 (1978-79), 88—99.

Studies on Immersion Education. Sacramento: California State Department of Education, 1984.

Sumiya, Mikio. "The Functions and Social Structure of Education: Schools and Japanese Society," *Journal of Social and Political Ideas in Japan,* Vol. 5 (December, 1967), 117—38.

Terrell, T. "The Natural Approach in Bilingual Education," in *Schooling and Language Minority Students: A Theoretical Framework.* Developed by the California State Department of Education, Office of Bilingual Bicultural Education. Los Angeles: Evaluation, Dissemination and Assessment Center, California State University, Los Angeles, 1981.

Treat, Payson J. *Diplomatic Relations Between the United States and Japan, 1853—1905.* In three volumes. Magnolia, Mass.: Peter Smith Publisher, Inc., 1963.

Ueda, Keiko. "Sixteen Ways to Avoid Saying 'No' in Japan: A Survey of the Function and Frequency of Japanese Patterns of Declining Requests." English abstract in *Patterns of Communication In and Out of Japan.* Edited by Mayumi Hara. Tokyo: International Christian University, 1974.

Wilson, Robert A., and Bill Hosokawa. *East to America: A History of the Japanese in the United States.* New York: William Morrow and Company, Inc., 1982.

Suggested Readings

Befu, Harumi. *Japan: An Anthropological Introduction.* Culture Area Series. New York: Harper and Row Publications, Inc., 1971. This work, especially Chapter 5 on class, work, and education and Chapter 6 on ethos might interest educators.

Benedict, Ruth. *The Chrysanthemum and the Sword: Patterns of Japanese Culture.* New York: New American Library, 1967. This is a classic work on traditional values.

Doi, Takeo. *The Anatomy of Dependence* (Fifth printing). Translated by John Bester from Japanese. New York: Kodansha International USA, Ltd., 1973. The author, a psychologist, posits the view that dependency relations are the emotional and structural cement of Japanese society.

Fukutake, Tadashi. *Japanese Society Today* (Second edition). New York: Columbia University Press, 1981.

Hadamitzky, Wolfgang, and Mark Spahn. *Kanji and Kana: A Handbook and Dictionary of the Japanese Writing System.* Rutland, Vt., and Tokyo: Charles E. Tuttle Co., Inc., 1981. The introduction includes a good explanation of the Japanese writing system.

Hane, Mikiso. *Peasants, Rebels and Outcasts: The Underside of Modern Japan.* New York: Pantheon Books, 1982. This book contains vivid stories of the hardships of modernization from the 1880s to the 1940s.

Henkin, W.A. "Toward Counseling the Japanese in America: A Crosscultural Primer," *Journal of Counseling and Development,* Vol. 63 (April, 1985), 500—3.

Hoopes, David. *Global Guide to International Education.* New York: Facts on File, Inc., 1984.

Jordan, Eleanor H., and Hamako Ito Chaplin. *Reading Japanese.* Linguistic Series. Rutland, Vt., and Tokyo: Charles E. Tuttle Co., Inc. 1976.

Kikumura, Akemi. *Through Harsh Winters: The Life of a Japanese Immigrant Woman.* Novato, Calif.: Chandler and Sharp Publications, Inc., 1981.

Kitano, Harry H. *Japanese Americans: The Evolution of a Subculture* (Second edition). Ethnic Groups in American Life Series. Englewood Cliffs, N.J.: Prentice-Hall, Inc., 1976. This book covers the period from the earliest immigration of Japanese up to 1970s.

Kobayashi, H. "Rhetorical Patterns in English and Japanese," *TESOL Quarterly,* Vol. 18 (December, 1984), 737—38.

Minoura, Y. *Life In-Between: The Acquisition of Cultural Identity Among Japanese Children Living in the United States.* Los Angeles: University of California, 1979 (unpublished doctoral dissertation).

Nakane, Chie. *Japanese Society.* Berkeley: University of California Press, 1985. This work gives a sociologist's view of the hierarchical structure of human relations in Japan.

Naotsuka, Reiko, and Nancy Sakamoto. *Mutual Understanding of Different Cultures* (ISBN 4-469-24063-X). Tokyo: Taishukan Publishing Co., 1985. A careful analysis of Japanese and English speakers' ways of expressing greetings, thanks, concerns, and complaints, and the misperceptions that result from literal translation of such expressions across the two languages.

Opening Doors: Contemporary Japan. New York: The Asia Society, 1979.

Rebischung, James. *Japan: The Facts of Modern Business and Social Life* (Fourth printing). Rutland, Vt., and Tokyo: Charles E. Tuttle Co., Inc., 1982.

Reischauer, Edwin O. *Japan: The Story of a Nation* (Revised edition). New York: Alfred A. Knopf, Inc., 1974.

Reischauer, Edwin O. *The Japanese.* Cambridge: Harvard University Press, 1977.

Rescorla, L., and S. Okuda. "Lexical Development in Second Language Acquisition: Initial Stages in a Japanese Child's Learning of English," *Journal of Child Language,* Vol. 11 (October, 1984), 689—95.

Rohlen, Thomas P. *Japan's High Schools.* Center for Japanese Studies, University of California, Berkeley, Series. Berkeley and Los Angeles: University of California Press, 1983. This work describes five high schools in a large city and covers the history of public education in Japan, university entrance examinations, the organization of schools, political issues in education, classroom instruction, and adolescence.

Sato, Ester M.; Loren I. Shishido; and Masako Sakihara. *Japanese Now,* Vol. I. Honolulu: University of Hawaii Press, 1982.

Sheridan, E.M. "Early Reading in Japan," *Reading World,* Vol. 21 (May, 1982) 326—32.

Smith, Bradley. *Japan: A History in Art.* Garden City, New York: Doubleday, 1971. The colorful woodblocks depicting the new meeting of Western and Japanese cultures at the end of the nineteenth century are especially interesting.

Takemoto, S. "Cultural Implications of Language Contrasts Between Japanese and English," *International Review of Applied Linguistics in Language Teaching,* Vol. 20 (November, 1982), 263—78.

Tomine, S. "Jan Ken Po Gakkō: A Japanese-American Cultural Education Program," *Journal of Multicultural Counseling and Development,* Vol. 13 (October, 1985), 164—69.

Vogel, Ezra F. *Japan As Number One: Lessons for America.* Cambridge: Harvard University Press, 1979. This book emphasizes the "group-directed quest for knowledge" as an organizing principle of civic and business life in Japan.

Appendix A

Districts Ranked by Enrollment of Limited-English-Proficient Students Who Speak Japanese

California law requires that school districts each year conduct a language census. The purpose of the census is to identify students who are considered to be limited-English proficient (LEP). Once identified, state law requires that LEP students be offered bilingual learning opportunities.

In the spring, 1986, 10,599 students were reported to speak Japanese at home. Of these students, 3,946 or 37 percent were found to be of limited-English proficiency and were classified as LEP.

In addition to the 32 districts listed below that enroll 23 or more LEP Japanese-speaking students, another 239 districts reported between 1 and 22 LEP students who speak Japanese.

Districts Ranked by Enrollment of LEP Students Who Speak Japanese, Spring, 1986*

Name of school district	Rank by number of LEP (Japanese) students	Number of (Japanese) students	LEP (Japanese) students as a percentage of state LEP (Japanese) students
Torrance Unified	1	534	13.5
Los Angeles Unified	2	399	10.1
Palos Verdes Peninsula Unified	3	266	6.7
Irvine Unified	4	166	4.2
San Francisco Unified	5	131	3.3
Alhambra City Elementary	6	111	2.8
San Mateo City Elementary	7	96	2.4
Cupertino Union Elementary	8	88	2.2
San Diego Unified	9	82	2.1
Millbrae Elementary	10	74	1.9
San Mateo Union High	11	67	1.7
Arcadia Unified	12	59	1.5
San Marino Unified	13	49	1.2

*Source: "DATA BICAL Report No. 86-7H." Sacramento: California State Department of Education, Office of Bilingual Education, spring, 1986

Name of school district	Rank by number of LEP (Japanese) students	Number of LEP (Japanese) students	LEP (Japanese) students as a percentage of state LEP (Japanese) students
Richmond Unified	14	46	1.2
Hacienda La Puente Unified	15	46	1.2
Glendale Unified	16	42	1.1
Fremont Unified	17	41	1.0
ABC Unified	18	40	1.0
San Gabriel Elementary	19	39	1.0
Santa Clara Unified	20	39	1.0
South Pasadena Unified	21	38	1.0
Palo Alto City Unified	22	38	1.0
Burlingame Elementary	23	34	0.9
Fullerton Elementary	24	32	0.8
Santa Monica-Malibu Unified	25	29	0.7
Chula Vista City Elementary	26	29	0.7
La Canada Unified	27	26	0.7
Sacramento City Unified	28	25	0.6
Sunnyvale Elementary	29	24	0.6
Garden Grove Unified	30	23	0.6
Poway City Unified	31	23	0.6
Oak Grove Elementary	32	23	0.6

Appendix B
Educational Resources

Japanese Publications on Japanese-English Bilingual Education

A source of studies of bilingual children, curricular ideas, and Japanese language ability tests designed for Japanese-speaking children who have been educated for some years outside Japan. All materials are in Japanese and designed for special "bilingual" programs in Japan for returning Japanese students.

The Center for Education of Children Overseas
Tokyo Gakugei University
4-1-1 Nikui Kita-Machi, Koganei-shi,
Tokyo 184 Japan

National Clearinghouse for Bilingual Education

The National Clearinghouse maintains a current "Information Packet for Japanese Bilingual Programs" that lists current sources of materials, interested organizations, and bibliographic references of value to Japanese bilingual programs. They always welcome additional tips as to new or overlooked resources. The "Information Packet" is free.

National Clearinghouse for
  Bilingual Education
COMSIS Corporation
11501 Georgia Ave., Suite 102
Silver Spring, MD 20902
(800) 647-0123

Sources of Information About Japan

ARC Associates, Inc.
310 Eight Street., Suite 305A
Oakland, CA 94607
(415) 834-9455

Asian American Resource Center
California State University,
  Los Angeles
5151 State University Drive
Los Angeles, CA 90032
(213) 224-2220

Center for Japanese American Studies
3232 Campbell Hall
University of California, Los Angeles
Los Angeles, CA 90024-1546
(213) 825-2975

Country/Culture Profiles
National Association for Foreign
  Student Affairs
Committee on Foreign Students
1860 19th St., N.W.
Washington, DC 20009

Culturgram on Japan
Publications Services
280 HRCB
Brigham Young University
Provo, UT 84602

East Asian Studies Center
University of Southern California
Los Angeles, CA 90089-0044
(213) 743-5080

Institute for East Asian Studies
University of California, Berkeley
2223 Fulton Street
Berkeley, CA 94720
(415) 642-2809

Institute for Intercultural Studies
11729 Gateway Blvd.
Los Angeles, CA 90064
(213) 479-6045

Institute of Far Eastern Studies
Seton Hall University
162 South Orange Ave.
South Orange, NJ 07079
(201) 762-4973

International Internship Programs
401 Colman Building
811 First Ave.
Seattle, WA 98104

The Japan-U.S. Senate Scholarship
 Program
Youth for Understanding
International Center
Program Administration Department
3501 Newark St., N.W.
Washington, DC 20016

Videotapes on Japan
The Asia Society
Education and Communications
725 Park Ave.
New York, NY 10021
(212) 288-6400

Materials Used for Teaching Japanese

Alfonso, Anthony; Sumiko Gotoo; and Solrun Hoaas. *Alfonso Japanese.* Canberra, Australia: Curriculum Development Center (Mailing address: P.O. Box 632, Manuka, A.C.T. 2603), 1977.

A five-book series for secondary students of Japanese. Tapes and a teacher's handbook are available. Books include activities for developing listening, speaking, reading, and writing skills.

Introduction to Japanese Hiragana. Stanford, Calif.: Stanford Program on International and Crosscultural Education.

An introduction to the Japanese writing syllabary and the basic sounds of the Japanese language. A pronunciation tape is included.

Japanese Language Educational Videotape Series. New York: TeleJapan USA, Inc. (Mailing address: 964 Third Ave., New York, NY 10155). Telephone (212) 980-5333.

A series of videotapes for beginning students in the Japanese language. A student's textbook and a teaching guide are available.

Kimizuka, Sumako, and others. *Oral Language Lessons for the Elementary Grades.* Los Angeles: Los Angeles Unified School District, Trilingual Magnet School, 1983.

Lessons for students in kindergarten and grades one through six. A teacher's framework developed under a grant from the National Endowment for the Humanities is included.

Textbooks and instructional materials are available from the California Association of Japanese Language Schools, 1218 Menlo Ave., Los Angeles, CA 90006.

Bookstores

In California some of the best sources of books, magazines, and records in the Japanese language, English-language books on Japan, and language instruction textbooks and audiotapes in both languages are retail bookstores.

Kinokuniya Bookstore
Japan Center
1581 Webster St.
San Francisco, CA 94115
(415) 567-7625

Kinokuniya Bookstore
110 South Los Angeles St.
Los Angeles, CA 90012
(213) 687-4447

Kinokuniya Bookstore
Weller Court, Suite 106
123 South Weller St.
Los Angeles, CA 90012
(213) 687-4480

Kinokuniya Bookstore
2141 West 182nd St.
Torrance, CA 90504
(213) 327-6577

Rafu Bookstore
307 East First St.
Los Angeles, CA 90012
(213) 626-3977

Tokyo-Do Shoten
1630 West Redondo Beach
Gardena, CA 90247
(213) 770-4091

Japanese children's book also are available from publishers of *Fukuinkan Shoten* books. These books are distributed in northern California by Iaconi Family Book Imports. Publications include original Japanese stories, which are familiar in translation as English children's books, as well as Japanese versions of many classic stories from English and other languages. Picture books, science books, and periodical publications for children and parents are available. (A catalog is available.)

Iaconi Family Book Imports
300 Pennsylvania
San Francisco, CA 94107
(415) 285-7393

Resources for Teaching About Japan

The Japan Project/SPICE (Stanford Program on International and Crosscultural Education) is a curriculum and staff development project that assists precollegiate educators in teaching more effectively about Japan. The project publishes classroom-tested teaching materials on contemporary and historical Japan for elementary and high school levels. Project staff members are available for consultation and presentation assistance in staff development programs that are primarily for affiliates of the statewide network of international studies resource centers, organized under the auspices of the

California International Studies Project (CISP). The latter is a project begun in 1986 by Stanford University in cooperation with Global Educators and the World Affairs Council of Northern California, under the auspices of the State Department of Education.

The Japan Project/SPICE
Lou Henry Hoover Building, Room 200
Stanford University
Stanford, CA 94305
(415) 723-1116

An extensive resource on Japanese Americans is the Japanese Curriculum Project (JACP) in San Mateo. JACP has a wide selection of books, curriculum materials, audiovisual cassettes, and other teaching materials for the classroom. JACP was founded 15 years ago by educators in California who recognized the need to develop and disseminate curriculum materials on Japanese Americans. A catalog of available materials may be obtained from:

Japanese American Curriculum Project, Inc.
P.O. Box 367
414 East Third St.
San Mateo, CA 94401
(415) 343-9408

Japan Database: Resources on Japan for K—12 Education was developed by the Council of Chief State School Officers to provide information about Japan to elementary and high school educators. It contains five major categories of information: specialists on Japan and Japanese studies; sources of information on Japan; curriculum materials on Japan; activities about Japan; and exchange programs with Japan. Contact:

Japan Database Project
Council of Chief State School Officers
379 Hall of the States
400 North Capitol St., N.W.
Washington, D.C. 20001
(202) 393-8161

Another invaluable resource for teaching about Japan is the official Japan Information Service of the Consulate General of Japan in San Francisco and Los Angeles. The Japan Information Service distributes informational posters and pamphlets on Japan, lends films about Japan, and maintains a research and reference library of English and Japanese materials.

Japan Information Service
Consulate General of Japan,
 Los Angeles
250 East First St., Suite 1507
Los Angeles, CA 90012
(213) 624-8305

Japan Information Service
Consulate General of Japan,
 San Francisco
1737 Post St., Suite 4-5
San Francisco, CA 94115
(415) 921-8000

Resources for Teaching About Japanese Americans

The history of the Japanese people in America and current information on issues of interest to Japanese Americans are available from the Japanese American Citizens League (JACL). In particular, a resource manual entitled *The Experience of Japanese Americans in the United States: A Teacher's Resource Manual* provides facts and suggests activities and materials for increasing awareness among all students. It may be obtained from JACL.

Japanese American Citizens League
912 F St.
Fresno, CA 93706
(209) 237-4006

Japanese American Citizens League
244 South San Pedro, Room 507
Los Angeles, CA 90012
(213) 626-4471

Japanese American Citizens League/
National Headquarters
1765 Sutter St.
San Francisco, CA 94115
(415) 921-5225

The Japanese American Historical
Society of Southern California
1934 West 232nd St.
Torrance, CA 90501
(213) 326-0608

The Japanese American History Room
1840 Sutter St., Room 206
San Francisco, CA 94115
(415) 921-1485

The Japanese American Library
1759 Sutter St.
P.O. Box 590598
San Francisco, CA 94159-0598
(415) 567-5006

The Japanese American National
Museum
941 E. Third St., Suite 201
Los Angeles, CA 90013
(213) 625-0414

The National Japanese American
Historical Society
1855 Folsom St.
San Francisco, CA 94103
(415) 431-5007

Community Organizations

Asian American Communities for
Education
2012 Pine Street
San Francisco, CA 94115
(415) 921-5537

Japan America Society of Southern
California
244 South San Pedro
Los Angeles, CA 90012
(213) 687-3275

Japan National Tourist Organization
624 South Grand Ave., Suite 2640
Los Angeles, CA 90017
(213) 623-1952

Japan National Tourist Organization
360 Post St., Suite 401
San Francisco, CA 94108
(415) 989-7140

The Japan Society of Northern
California
312 Sutter St., Suite 406
San Francisco, CA 94108
(415) 986-4383

Japan Travel Bureau, International, Inc.
624 South Grand Ave.
Los Angeles, CA 90017
(213) 623-5629

Japan Travel Bureau, International, Inc.
360 Post St.
San Francisco, CA 94108
(415) 433-5907

Japanese Business Association
345 South Figueroa St., Suite 206
Los Angeles, CA 90071
(213) 485-0160

Japanese Chamber of Commerce of
Northern California
312 Sutter St.
San Francisco, CA 94108
(415) 986-6140

Japanese Chamber of Commerce for
Southern California
244 South San Pedro, Suite 504
Los Angeles, CA 90012
(213) 626-5116

Japanese Community Youth Council
2012 Pine St.
San Francisco, CA 94115
(415) 563-8052

Newspapers

Los Angeles

Cashu Mainichi
915 East First St.
Los Angeles, CA 90012
(213) 628-4686

Rafu Shimpo
259 South Los Angeles St.
Los Angeles, CA 90012
(213) 629-2231

San Francisco

Hokubei Mainichi
1746 Post St.
San Francisco, CA 94115
(415) 567-7324

Nichibei Times
2211 Bush St.
San Francisco, CA 94115
(415) 921-6820

Japanese Schools Supported by the Ministry of Education of Japan

The Japanese government helps support schools for Japanese-speaking students who must keep up with their Japanese studies for the day they will return to the Japanese school system. Classes are held in public school buildings on Saturdays.

Asahi Gakuen
244 South San Pedro St., Suite 308
Los Angeles, CA 90012
(213) 613-1325

Member Schools of the California Association of Japanese Language Schools, Inc.

Japanese Language School
Unified System
1218 Menlo Ave.
Los Angeles, CA 90006
(213) 383-4706

Northern Chapter

Rissho Gakuen
5191 24th St.
Sacramento, CA 95822
(916) 456-8371

Sakura Gakuen
2401 Riverside Blvd.
Sacramento, CA 95818
(916) 446-0121

Bay Area Chapter

Berkeley Japanese School
2121 Channing Way
Berkeley, CA 94704
(415) 524-9793

Monterey Peninsula JACL
   Japanese Language School
424 Adams St.
Monterey, CA 93940
(408) 899-2905

San Mateo Nippon Gakuen
2 S. Claremont
San Mateo, CA 94401
(415) 348-3178

Soko Gakuen
1881 Pine St.
San Francisco, CA 94109
(415) 355-6221

Southern Alameda County
   Buddhist Church Japanese
   Language School
32975 Alvarado-Niles Road
Union City, CA 94587
(415) 471-2581

Tri-City Japanese Language School
P.O. Box 262
Mountain View, CA 94042
(415) 341-7899

Southern Chapter

East-West Language School
16110 La Salle Ave.
Gardena, CA 90247
(213) 532-3770

Gardena Buddhist Church
Japanese Language School
1517 W. 166th St.
Gardena, CA 90247
(213) 327-9400

Gardena Valley
Japanese Language School
16215 S. Gramercy Pl.
Gardena, CA 90247-0903
(213) 324-6611

Japanese Mission Westminster
First Baptist Church
14200 Golden West
Westminster, CA 92683
(714) 892-2829

San Diego Japanese Language School
2624 Market St.
San Diego, CA 92102
(619) 233-5858

San Fernando Valley
Japanese Language Institute
12953 Branford St.
Pacoima, CA 91331
(818) 896-8612

UMC Japanese School
1444 W. Rosecrans
Gardena, CA 90247
(213) 323-8412

**Schools Directed by the Japanese
   Language School Unified System**

Hollywood Gakuen
3929 Middlebury St.
Los Angeles, CA 90028
(213) 664-2070

Junior and High School Department
1218 Menlo Ave.
Los Angeles, CA 90006
(213) 383-4706

Long Beach Gakuen
1766 Sea Bright Ave.
Long Beach, CA 90810
(213) 437-9924

Orange Coast Gakuen
c/o Coastline Community College
3101 Pacific View Dr.
Corona Del Mar, CA 92625

Pasadena Gakuen
595 Lincoln Ave.
Pasadena, CA 91103
(818) 356-9061

Rafu Chuo Gakuen
P.O. Box 33286
Los Angeles, CA 90033
(213) 268-4955

Rafu Daiichi Gakuen
3411 12th Ave.
Los Angeles, CA 90018
(213) 734-5289

Southeast Gakuen
14615 S. Gridley Road
Norwalk, CA 90650
(213) 863-5996

Valley Gakuen
8850 Lankershim Blvd.
Sun Valley, CA 91352
(818) 767-9279

Other Japanese Language Schools in California
(Partial Listing)

Alameda Japanese Language School
Alameda Buddhist Church
2325 Pacific Ave.
Alameda, CA 94501

Asahi Gakuen
152 N. Vermont Ave.
Los Angeles, CA 90004
(213) 628-2363, 387-6313

Berkeley Japanese School
2121 Channing Way
Berkeley, CA 94704

Community Language School
Calvary Presbyterian Church
1239 S. Monroe St.
Stockton, CA 95206
(209) 466-0221

Concord Japanese School
3165 Treat Blvd.
Concord, CA 94510
(415) 229-1659

Florin Japanese Language School
8320 Florin Road
Sacramento, CA 95828

Fowler Japanese School
Ninth Street
Fowler, CA 93625
(209) 834-2077

Fresno Japanese Language School
721 C St.
Fresno, CA 93706

Garden Grove Japanese Language
 School
10771 Sherman Way
Garden Grove, CA 92640
(714) 531-4150

Glendale Japanese Free
 Methodist Church
1800 Lake St.
Glendale, CA 91201
(818) 242-4738

Harbor City Koyasan
 Japanese School
1306 W. 253rd St.
Harbor City, CA 90710
(213) 624-1267

Institute for Intercultural Studies
 Language School
11729 Gateway Blvd.
Los Angeles, CA 90064
(213) 479-6045

Japanese Language School
Unified System
1218 Menlo Ave.
Los Angeles, CA 90006
(213) 383-4706

Kinmon Gakuen
2031 Bush St.
San Francisco, CA 94115

Lodi Japanese Language School
23 N. Stockton St.
Lodi, CA 95240

Marin Japanese School
Marin Buddhist Church
Miller Ave.
Mill Valley, CA 94941

Marysville Japanese Language School
c/o Marysville Buddhist Church
P.O. Box 1462
Marysville, CA 95901
(916) 743-6426

Monterey Japanese School
1159 Mono Court
Seaside, CA 93955
(408) 899-2905

Morgan Hill Japanese School
Morgan Hill Buddhist Building
16160 Murphy Ave.
Morgan Hill, CA 95037

Nishi Hongwanji Nihongo Gakko
815 E. First St.
Los Angeles, CA 90012
(213) 680-9130

Oakland Buddhist Church
Japanese Language School
825 Jackson St.
Oakland, CA 94607

Orange County Japanese School
c/o Orange County Buddhist Church
909 South Dale St.
Anaheim, CA 92804
(714) 827-9590

Otani Nihongo Gakuen
1534 Oregon St.
Berkeley, CA 94703

Oxnard Japanese Language School
c/o Oxnard Buddhist Church
250 South "H" St.
Oxnard, CA 93030
(805) 483-5948

Palo Alto Japanese School
2751 Louis Road
Palo Alto, CA 94303

Pasadena Japanese Language School
c/o Pasadena Buddhist Church
1993 Glen Ave.
Pasadena, CA 91103

Rafu Daini Gakuen
1035 South Fedora St.
Los Angeles, CA 90006

Salinas Nihongo Gakuen
14 California St.
Salinas, CA 93901

San Jose Nihongo Gakuen
San Jose Buddhist Church
640 North 5th St.
San Jose, CA 95112

Sanger Japanese Language School
Sanger Japanese American Citizens
 League
P.O. Box 386
"K" St.
Sanger, CA 93657

Santa Maria Japanese School
134 North Western Ave.
Santa Maria, CA 93454

Santo Kyokai Gakuen
Tri-City Buddhist Church
575 Stierlin Road
Mountain View, CA 94043

Sawtelle Japanese Language School
2110 Corinth Ave.
Los Angeles, CA 90025

Stockton Buddhist Church
2820 Shimizu Drive
Stockton, CA 95205
(209) 466-6701

Watsonville Buddhist Church
427 Bridge St.
Watsonville, CA 95076

West Covina Japanese School
1203 W. Puente Ave.
West Covina, CA 91790
(818) 962-0506

Appendix C
Course of Study for Japanese Language in Elementary Schools in Japan*

Overall Objectives

To develop the ability to accurately understand and express the Japanese language, to deepen the interest in the Japanese language, to develop the sense of language, and to cultivate an attitude of respect for the Japanese language

Objectives and Contents for Each Grade

First Grade

I. Objectives

- To enable pupils to write brief sentences on and to talk about what they have experienced and other things familiar to them, and to help them develop an attitude of willingness to express what they think about
- To help pupils acquire the ability to read with comprehension what is written and to listen to what is told, and to guide them to develop an attitude of willingness to enjoy reading

II. Contents—Linguistic Items

- To give instruction on the following linguistic items through the activities of A and B below in order to develop the basic ability of expression and understanding in the Japanese language:
  - To speak clearly without using infantile pronunciation
  - To pay attention to posture and mouth for clear pronunciation
  - To read and write *hiragana*
  - To read and write most of *katakana*
  - To read about 70 Chinese characters which are allocated to grade one in the "List of Chinese Characters Classified by Grade" and to write most of them
  - To use Chinese characters properly in a written sentence
  - To be able to indicate the sounds such as long-sound (*cho-on*), contracted-sound (*yo-on*), short-stressed-sound (*soku-on*) and

---

*Reprinted by permission from *Course of Study for Elementary Schools in Japan* (Notification 155). Tokyo: Ministry of Education, Science and Culture, 1983.

splash-sound (*hatsu-on*), and to write correctly in a sentence these auxiliary suffixes of *ha, he, o*
- To pay attention to the use of comma and period
- To pay attention to the use of square brackets
- To have interest in the phrases necessary for expression and understanding
- To have interest in the meaning of phrases and their usage
- To pay attention to the letters and phrases which are difficult to read and understand
- To read and write, paying attention to the correspondence between subject and predicate
- To become familiar with the sentence of honorific style
- To speak, paying attention to the two different styles of expression: polite and ordinary
- To give instruction on the following for copying characters:
  - To write carefully a character, paying attention to its shape and following the orthodox order of writing
  - To write a character correctly, paying attention to the prescribed form

A. Expression

1. To give instruction on the following in order to develop the ability of expression in the Japanese language:

   a. To think about or find out what is to be written in sentences
   b. To write about what has been experienced or what has been heard about, following the sequence of events involved
   c. To compose a simple sentence by combining words or a brief passage by connecting sentences, while continuing to give consideration to the subject
   d. To develop the habit of rereading the sentences and passages written by oneself and to be careful about mistakes made
   e. To express what is seen or what is heard as correctly as possible
   f. To speak about what has been experienced, following the sequence of events involved

B. Understanding

1. To give instruction on the following in order to develop the ability of understanding in the Japanese language:

   a. To read aloud with correct articulation
   b. To understand the essence of what is written
   c. To read, imaging the situation of a scene
   d. To grasp correctly the content of what has been told

Second Grade

I. Objectives

- To enable pupils to write passages on and to talk about the events in sequence, and to develop an attitude to express correctly
- To enable pupils to read passages and to listen to a story with the understanding of the passage of the events involved and changes in the situation, and to help them promote the willingness to read easy reading materials

II. Contents—Linguistic Items

- To give instruction on the following linguistic items through the activities of A and B below, in order to develop the basic ability of expression and understanding in the Japanese language:
  - To speak clearly with due attention to the pronunciation
  - To pay attention to posture and mouth for clear pronunciation
  - To read and write *katakana* and to understand the proper usage of *katakana* in a sentence or passage
  - To read about 220 Chinese characters which are allocated to grades one and two in the "List of Chinese Characters Classified by Grade" and to write most of them
  - To readily use, when writing sentences and passages, those Chinese characters already learned
  - To use correctly in a sentence the auxiliary suffixes of *ha, he, o* and to pay attention to the use of *kana*
  - To write passages, using the period correctly with due attention to the use of the comma
  - To grasp how to use in the square brackets [   ] and to use them correctly in passages
  - To increase the number of letters and phrases required to express and understand
  - To notice that there are phrases which have similar and opposite meanings or meanings in contrast
  - To read and write sentences, paying attention to the correspondence between subject and predicate and to the relationship between modifier and the modified '
  - To read and write passages, paying attention to the continuation between sentences
  - To notice functions and usages of demonstrative and conjunction in a sentence or passage
  - To become used to the passage of honorific style
  - To understand the difference in the usage between the polite and ordinary words
- To give instruction on the following for copying characters:
  - To write carefully a character, paying attention to its shape and following the orthodox order of writing

– To write a character correctly, paying attention to the border, intersection, and direction of strokes

A. Expression
  1. To give instruction on the following in order to develop the ability of expression in the Japanese language:
    a. To select items necessary for the subject to write about
    b. To write and speak about the subject, putting its contents in sequence
    c. To compose a passage, paying attention to the linkage of sentences for the reader's easy understanding of the subject
    d. To develop the habit of correcting mistakes made, through rereading passages written by oneself
    e. To express what is seen or what is heard as correctly as possible
    f. To speak about what has been experienced, following the sequence of events involved

B. Understanding
  1. To give instruction on the following in order to develop the ability of understanding in the Japanese language:
    a. To read aloud, considering the content of a passage to read
    b. To read or listen to a story, considering the chronological order of events involved, changes in the situation, and the sequence of the events
    c. To read, imaging the characters and the scenes involved
    d. To point out letters impossible to read, phrases hard to understand, and parts impossible to understand
    e. To try to grasp correctly the content, following the expressions made in a passage
    f. To grasp the content of a passage correctly, while listening to it

Third Grade

I. Objectives
- To enable pupils to write a passage, or to tell a story, of simple composition on a certain item so that the main point can be understood and to develop an attitude to express (themselves) in an easily understandable manner.
- To enable pupils to read a passage or to listen to a story with the right understanding of the main points of the content and to develop an attitude to willingly read a wide variety of reading materials

II. Contents—Linguistic Items
- To give instruction on the following linguistic items through the activities of A and B below, in order to develop the basic ability of expression and understanding in the Japanese language:

- To speak, while trying to correct the local dialect or personal wrong habits in pronunciation, if any
- To know about the kinds of words to be written in *katakana* and to use them properly in a sentence or passage
- To read about 410 Chinese characters that are allocated to grades one to three in the "List of Chinese Characters Classified by Grade" and to write most of them
- To use correctly those Chinese characters already learned in writing passages
- To write with due attention to *okurigana* and to notice the conjugation
- To understand the function of the comma and to write a passage using commas at necessary places
- To use properly the square brackets [ ] and to understand how to use other important symbols, too
- To increase the number of letters and words required to express and understand
- To know the functions and relations of words in a passage and to notice that the words are classified by nature
- To read and write a sentence with clear understanding of the relationship between subject and predicate and also of the relationship between modifier and the modified
- To read and write a passage with attention to the conjunctive relationship between the sentences
- To pay attention to the functions and usages of the demonstrative and the conjunction in a sentence or passaage
- To write with due attention to the difference between the honorific and ordinary styles
- To use polite words in accordance with the person to talk or the given situation

- To give instruction on the following for copying characters:
  - To write letters correctly, following the orthodox order of writing
  - To write letters in a right shape, paying attention to the formation of each letter
  - To write letters carefully, using a writing brush, paying attention to the strokes such as length of stroke, starting point, turning point, closing point, and so forth

  A. Expression
  1. To give instruction on the following in order to develop the ability of expression in the Japanese language:
     a. To select items necessary for writing a passage and to write it by arranging items in sequence
     b. To write, considering focus and pause of item to be expressed, and to speak, considering the point of story, in order to make the content easily understandable
     c. To write after thoroughly observing what is to be written

      d. To compose a passage, paying attention to the linkage of sentences for the reader's easy understanding of the content

      e. To use words properly in a passage, in accordance with their meanings and functions

      f. To reread passages written by oneself and to correct mistakes made

      g. To express what is seen or what is heard as correctly as possible

      h. To try to find materials to be written from among what has been heard or read and to write

      i. To speak in sequence

B. Understanding

   1. To give instruction on the following in order to develop the ability of understanding in the Japanese language:

      a. To read aloud, using techniques to express the content of passage

      b. To understand the major points of a passage or story and to summarize them from one's own standpoint

      c. To state the impression on the content of a story that has been read and to think from one's own standpoint about the behavior of the personality in the story

      d. To discuss the content of a story that has been read and to pay attention to the individual differences in ways of feeling and thinking

      e. To understand what seems important from one's own standpoint

      f. To read, imagining the sentiments of characters and scenes of situation involved

      g. To think about the meaning of words in the context of a story

      h. To develop the habit of grasping the content expressed in accordance with the expression given in a passage

      i. To write passages by arranging the content in order to understand the content and to utilize (them) for one's own expression

      j. To notice the parts of good expression and to try to use them in one's own writing

      k. To grasp the content of a story correctly, while listening to it

Fourth Grade

I. Objectives

- To enable pupils to write passages in consideration of the formation and mutual relationship of paragraphs so as to make the central point to be expressed clearly, to speak in consideration of the sequence of the content and degree of importance, and to develop an attitude to express in arranging the content

- To enable pupils to read correctly a sequence of passages, grasping the mutual relation between the major points of the paragraphs and their focal points, to listen to a story with the correct understanding of its central and other important points, and to increase the volume of their reading

II. Contents—Linguistic Items

- To give instruction on the following linguistic items through the activities of A and B below in order to develop the basic ability of expressions and understanding in the Japanese language.

  - To speak correctly without using dialect or personal wrong habits in pronunciation
  - To speak at proper speed and loudness in accordance with the purpose of speech
  - To read about 610 Chinese characters which are allocated to grades one to four in the "List of Chinese Characters Classified by Grade" and to write most of them
  - To use correctly those Chinese characters already learned in writing passages
  - To write with due attention to *okurigana* and to be aware of the conjugation
  - To use punctuation marks properly and to write, starting on a new line, such portions as the beginning of a new paragraph and conversation
  - To increase the number of words necessary for expression and understanding
  - To understand how to compose words
  - To understand how to consult a dictionary for investigation about letters and words which are needed for expression and understanding
  - To deepen the understanding of the roles played by words in passages and their conjunctive relationship and to know the characteristics of classified words
  - To obtain elementary understanding of sentence structure
  - To understand the elementary method of constructing a passage by understanding the conjunction relation between sentences and the mutual relation between paragraphs
  - To use properly demonstrative and conjunction, considering the relationship of meanings between sentences
  - To understand the difference between the honorific and ordinary styles of passage
  - To use polite words properly whenever necessary
  - To understand the difference between the standard language and dialects and to speak in standard language whenever necessary
  - To read Roman letters, to indicate simple words used in daily life, and to write in Roman letters

- To give instruction on the following for copying characters:
    - To write letters in a right shape, paying attention to the formation of each letter
    - To write letters so as to make them easily read, paying attention to their size and layout
    - To write letters correctly, using a writing brush, paying attention to the border, intersection, and direction of strokes

A. Expression
1. To give instruction on the following in order to develop the ability of expression in the Japanese language:
    a. To write passages after making one's ideas clear or putting them in order
    b. To develop a habit to decide what to write before writing
    c. To write in such a way as to make the central point of what is to be written clear and to speak in such a way as to make the central point of the content easily understandable
    d. To write matters in passage objectively
    e. To write in proper consideration of the structure of paragraphs and the linkage of paragraphs for the reader's easy understanding of the content
    f. To write sentences, paying attention to usage of words
    g. To reread what has been written by oneself, to correct any mistakes made, and to polish up as best as possible
    h. To write passages drawing subject-matter from what is read or what is heard
    i. To speak in logical sequence

B. Understanding
1. To give instruction on the following in order to develop the ability of understanding in Japanese language:
    a. To read aloud so as to make the listeners understand clearly the meaning of the items involved, the scenes, and the changes of the feeling of characters in the story
    b. To extract and describe the essence of a passage or of a story
    c. To understand the individual differences in understanding by making a comparison of impression on the content of what has been read or what has been heard about
    d. To summarize the important items involved in the light of the objectives of the reading and to read stories, paying attention to the details of its parts, if necessary
    e. To imagine the situation and the scene according to the description
    f. To understand the meaning of words in the context of a story

g. To read and understand correctly the content expressed according to the expression given in a paragraph

h. To copy exemplary sentences and to use such ways of expression in one's own writing

i. To read sentences, summarizing their content by paragraph, in order to understand them more correctly and more deeply, and to think about the relationships between paragraphs as well as between paragraph and whole passage

j. To read passages, while recognizing the differences in expression among the central and other matters of the content and to utilize the understanding in one's own writing

k. To grasp the content correctly, while listening to it

Fifth Grade

I. Objectives

- To enable pupils to write passages in consideration of the structure of the whole sentences and to talk about a story logically, so as to express their central theme and main points clearly, and to develop an attitude to express, keeping in view the other parts and the situation of a scene involved

- To enable pupils to read passages and to listen to a story while understanding their central theme and major points and to increase the pupils' knowledge and enrich their sentiments through reading

II. Contents—Linguistic Items

- To provide instruction on the following linguistic items through the activities of A and B below in order to develop the basic ability of expression and understanding in the Japanese language:

  - To speak with correct pronunciation
  - To speak, paying attention to the intonation and accent
  - To read about 800 Chinese characters which are allocated to grades one to five in the "List of Chinese Characters Classified by Grade" and to write most of them
  - To understand the function played by Chinese characters in a passage and to use them properly in a passage
  - To acquire elementary knowledge about the origin, characteristics, and composition of Chinese characters
  - To write a sentence correctly, paying attention to *okurigana* and *kana-zukai*
  - To write passages by proper use of punctuation marks and of new line
  - To expand the scope of words necessary for expression and understanding
  - To have interest in the word-feeling and sense of language in the use of words

- To become familiar with old literary expressions by reading easy passages in old literary style
- To understand the various functions played by words in terms of their usage in a passage
- To consult a dictionary for investigation about words which are needed for expression and understanding
- To understand the ways of correlating and contrasting words in a sentence and to understand that there are many ways of composing a sentence
- To deepen the understanding of the conjunctive relation between sentences and the mutual relation of one paragraph to another in a sequence of sentences and to deepen the understanding of the ways of passage composition
- To use properly the demonstrative and conjunctive words according to the relation of meanings between sentences
- To write distinctively in honorific and ordinary styles
- To use correctly honorific expressions which are frequently used in everyday life
- To speak in standard language, whenever necessary

- To give instruction on the following for copying characters:
  - To assess the shape, size, and layout of characters written and to utilize this knowledge when copying characters
  - To write letters correctly and orderly, using a writing brush, paying attention to the composition of letters.

A. Expression

- To give instruction on the following in order to develop the ability of expression in the Japanese language:
  a. To make one's own ideas clear by means of writing a passage
  b. To write passages about the necessary items arranged in accordance with the viewpoints and to utilize such ability in life and study
  c. To write a passage whose theme and substance are clear, and to speak in logical sequence
  d. To write passages, differentiating the facts from impressions and opinions
  e. To write passages that are distinctive in paragraph composition for the reader's easy understanding of the content and to write passages with logical sequence between paragraphs
  f. To write passages with due attention to the sentence structure and proper use of words
  g. To reread a passage written by oneself and to improve it in its way of description
  h. To write passages after selecting materials from what has been heard or read and making reference to the ways of description found in what has been read

       i. To read aloud in order to convey the content to other people

       j. To speak properly according to the purpose and intention

B. Understanding

- To give instruction on the following in order to develop the ability of understanding in Japanese language:

    a. To summarize one's impression and opinion with accurate understanding of the theme and substance concerned

    b. To read passages, grasping the writer's ways of viewing, thinking, and feeling

    c. To read passages for investigation of necessary matter or for collection of necessary information

    d. To understand correctly the meaning of words in the context of a copy

    e. To read and understand the content, paying attention to the details of a sentence and passage in accordance with the expression

    f. To read, appreciating the part of description where the feeling of the character involved or the scene of a situation is expressed

    g. To listen to a story so as to restructure its content from one's standpoint

    h. To deepen the understanding and appreciation of passages by means of copying exemplary sentences and to use the best points found in these sentences in one's own writing

    i. To understand the structure of whole passage in order to understand properly the content and to utilize it in one's expression

    j. To listen to a story accurately, and to understand the speaker's way of thinking

Sixth Grade

I. Objectives

- To enable pupils to write a passage or to tell a story suitable for the purpose and content of what is to be expressed and to develop an attitude to express properly and effectively
- To enable pupils to read passages in a proper way according to the purpose of reading, the style and form of sentences to be read, and to listen to a story effectively according to the purpose, and to develop a habit of selecting and reading appropriate reading materials

II. Contents—Linguistic Items

- To give instruction on the following linguistic items through the activities of A and B below in order to develop the basic ability of expression and understanding in the Japanese language:

- To speak with correct pronunciation
- To speak, paying attention to the intonation and accent
- To read about 1,000 Chinese characters which are allocated to grades one to six in the "List of Chinese Characters Classified by Grade" and to write most of them
- To deepen the understanding of the functions played by Chinese characters in modern passages which are in the form of mixing both Chinese characters and *kana* and to use properly those Chinese characters already learned
- To deepen the understanding of the origin and characteristics of *kana* and Chinese characters
- To write a sentence, paying attention to *okurigana,* and to write in correct *kana-zukai*
- To deepen the understanding of the structure and changes in words
- To increase the number of and to expand the scope of words necessary for expression and understanding
- To deepen the interest in the word-feeling and the sense of language in the use of words
- To become familiar with old literary expressions by reading easy passages in old literary style
- To deepen the understanding of the functions played by particles and auxiliary verbs in a sentence
- To have an interest in the origin of words
- To acquire a habit of consulting a dictionary for investigation about words which are needed for expression and understanding
- To read passages, paying attention to the mutual relationship of words used for the purpose of contrast in the whole sentences
- To deepen the understanding of the structure of a sentence and passage
- To write distinctively in honorific and ordinary styles in accordance with the purpose of writing
- To become familiar with the usage of honorific expressions in everyday life
- To speak in standard language, whenever necessary

- To give instruction on the following for copying characters:
  - To write a character, paying attention to its shape, size, and layout
  - To write letters properly, using a writing brush, paying attention to the shape and size of letters

  A. Expression

  - To give instruction on the following in order to develop the ability of expression in the Japanese language:

    a. To deepen one's thinking by writing passages
    b. To write passages in accordance with the purpose of writing without missing necessary matters and to utilize such ability in life and study

    c. To clarify the reference points and, on the basis of these, to state one's view and contention

    d. To write passages briefly or in detail according to the purpose of writing, keeping in view the structure of the whole passage

    e. To write passages, differentiating the facts from impressions and opinions, in accordance with the purpose

    f. To utilize effectively sentence and passage composition and usage of words in accordance with the purpose

    g. To reread a passage written by oneself and to consider more effective ways of description

    h. To write passages, summarizing or elaborating the content of sentences and items

    i. To read aloud so as to enable the listener to appreciate the content of what is read

    j. To speak properly in accordance with the purpose and intention

B. Understanding

- To give instruction on the following in order to develop the ability of understanding in the Japanese language:

    a. To read in a way to compare the content of passages with one's life and opinions

    b. To read in a way to clarify one's assessment concerning the writer's viewpoint, ways of thinking, and feeling

    c. To think how one's ways of feeling or thinking have changed as a result of reading a book or listening to a story

    d. To select appropriate books and to consider more effective ways of reading in accordance with the purpose

    e. To understand correctly the meaning of words in the context of a story

    f. To understand distinctively the objective description on facts and the impressions or opinions of the speaker or the writer

    g. To appreciate while reading portions of excellent depiction and description

    h. To write and speak, reconstructing the content of passage that already has been understood, in accordance with the purpose

    i. To think about why the writer has written briefly in some portions and in detail in others in order to use such knowledge for writing one's own writing

    j. To think about the ways that the writer has devised for describing the theme and substance of his writing and to use such knowledge for one's own writing

    k. To listen to a story and to understand accurately the speaker's thinking

Preparation of the Teaching Program and Points for Special Consideration in Teaching Through All Six Grades

In preparing the teaching program, the instructor should consider the following items:

1. Concerning the instruction on the items indicated in the Contents in each grade, appropriate language activities suitable for the developmental stage of the pupils in each grade should be selected and learning activities should be organized by combining these language activities.
2. Concerning the items indicated in the Contents for each grade, consideration can be made, if necessary, to teach them in an elementary manner in the preceding grade or in an advanced manner in the following grade.
3. Concerning A and B of the Contents for each grade, consideration should be given to selecting appropriate topics or materials and to giving instruction correlatively on the items indicated in A and B. Also, the abilities to express and understand should be developed in balance.
4. Concerning the instruction on composition in A of the Contents for each grade, emphasis should be placed on the development of the basic ability to make expression in passages as well as the improvement of the ability to think. Furthermore, approximately three-tenths of the total school hours allotted to the subject of the Japanese language should be spent for the composition works, and at the same time as many opportunities as possible should be provided for writing practice.
5. Concerning the instruction on reading in B of the contents for each grade, consideration should be given to encouraging the pupils to perform the reading activity positively in daily life, and at the same time, instruction should be provided in relation to instruction on reading in other subjects as well as in the school library. Moreover, a variety of books for the pupils should be selected, without any inclination to particular kinds, for the development of desirable personality.
6. Concerning the instruction on composition and copying characters, particular instruction on composition/calligraphy alone may be organized in accordance with the actual class conditions concerned and the effect of the instruction.

Instruction on linguistic items should be given as follows:

1. Among items concerning language, as far as those on pronunciation, letters, and grammar, as well as basic items for expression and understanding abilities are concerned, those requiring repeated practice and learning should be taken up separately.
2. Instruction on copying characters with a writing brush should be provided from grade three and above. Instruction should also be provided to develop the pupils' basic ability to copy with a hard pen and to write characters correctly and in right order. Moreover, the number of school hours allotted for the instruction on copying with

a writing brush should be approximately 20 school hours per year for each grade.

3. For instruction on Chinese characters, the shape of Chinese characters indicated in the "List of Chinese Characters Classified by Grade" should be regarded as the standard.

List of Chinese Characters Classified by Grade

GRADE 1	一 右 雨 円 王 音 下 火 花 学 気 九 休 金 空 月 犬 見 五 口 校 左 三 山 子 四 糸 字 耳 七 車 手 十 出 女 小 上 森 人 水 正 生 青 夕 石 赤 千 川 先 早 足 村 大 男 中 虫 町 天 田 土 二 日 入 年 白 八 百 文 木 本 名 目 立 力 林 六 (76 char-acters)
GRADE 2	引 雲 遠 何 科 夏 家 歌 画 回 会 海 絵 貝 外 間 顔 汽 記 帰 牛 魚 京 教 強 玉 近 形 計 元 原 戸 古 午 後 語 工 広 交 光 行 考 高 黄 合 谷 国 黒 今 才 作 算 止 市 思 紙 寺 自 時 室 社 弱 首 秋 春 書 少 場 色 食 心 新 親 図 数 西 声 星 晴 切 雪 船 前 組 走 草 多 太 体 台 池 地 知 竹 茶 昼 長 鳥 朝 通 弟 店 点 電 冬 刀 当 東 答 頭 同 道 読 南 馬 買 売 麦 半 番 父 風 分 聞 米 歩 母 方 北 毎 妹 明 鳴 毛 門 夜 野 友 用 曜 来 楽 里 理 話 (145 characters)
GRADE 3	悪 安 暗 医 意 育 員 院 飲 運 泳 駅 園 横 屋 温 化 荷 界 開 階 角 活 寒 感 館 岸 岩 起 期 客 究 急 級 宮 球 去 橋 業 曲 局 銀 苦 具 君 兄 係 軽 血 決 県 研 言 庫 湖 公 向 幸 港 号 根 祭 細 仕 死 使 始 指 歯 詩 次 事 持 式 実 写 者 主 守 取 酒 受 州 拾 終 習 週 集 住 重 所 暑 助 昭 消 尚 章 勝 乗 植 申 身 神 深 進 世 整 線 全 送 息 族 他 打 対 待 代 第 題 炭 短 着 注 柱 帳 調 直 追 丁 定 庭 鉄 転 都 度 投 島 湯 登 等 動 童 内 肉 農 波 配 畑 発 反 坂 板 皮 悲 美 鼻 氷 表 秒 病 品 員 部 服 福 物 平 返 勉 放 万 味 命 面 問 役 薬 由 油 有 遊 予 洋 葉 陽 様 落 流 旅 両 緑 礼 列 路 和 (195 characters)

115

	愛案衣以囲位委胃印英栄塩央億加貨課芽改械 害各覚完官漢管関観願希季紀喜旗器機議求救 給挙漁共協鏡競極区軍郡型景芸欠結建健験固 功候航康告差菜最材昨刷殺察参散産残士氏史 司姉試辞失借種周宿順初省唱照賞焼臣信真成 清勢静席積折節説浅戦選然争相倉想象速側統 卒孫帯隊達単談治置貯腸低底停的典伝徒努燈 堂働毒熱念敗倍博飯飛費必筆票標不夫付府副 粉兵別辺変便包法望牧末満脈民約勇要養浴利 陸良料量輪類令冷例歴連練老労録 (195 characters)
	圧易移因永営衛益液演往応恩仮果河過価賀快 解格確額刊幹慣歓眼基寄規技義逆久旧居許境 興均禁句訓群経潔件券険検絹限現減故個護効 厚耕構講鉱混査再災妻採際在財罪雑蚕酸賛支 示志師資似児識貧舎謝授収修衆祝述術準序除 招承称証条状常情織職制性政精製税責績接設 舌絶銭善祖素総造像増則測属損退貸態団断築 張提程敵適統銅導特得徳独任燃能破犯判版比 非肥備俵評貧布婦富武復複仏編弁保墓報豊防 貿暴未務無迷綿輸余預容率略留領 (195 characters)

GRADE 6																			
異	道	域	壱	宇	羽	映	延	沿	可	我	灰	街	革	拡	閣	割	株	干	巻
看	勧	簡	丸	危	机	揮	貴	疑	弓	吸	泣	供	胸	郷	勤	筋	系	径	敬
警	劇	穴	兼	憲	権	源	厳	己	呼	誤	后	好	孝	皇	紅	降	鋼	刻	穀
骨	困	砂	座	済	裁	策	冊	至	私	姿	視	詞	誌	磁	射	捨	尺	釈	若
需	樹	宗	就	従	縦	縮	熟	純	処	署	諸	将	笑	傷	障	城	蒸	針	仁
垂	推	寸	是	聖	誠	宣	専	染	泉	洗	奏	窓	創	層	操	蔵	臓	俗	存
尊	宅	担	探	段	暖	値	仲	宙	忠	著	庁	兆	頂	潮	賃	痛	辰	党	討
糖	届	難	弐	乳	認	納	脳	派	拝	肺	背	俳	班	晩	否	批	秘	腹	奮
陛	閉	片	補	宝	訪	亡	忘	棒	枚	幕	密	盟	模	矢	訳	郵	優	幼	羊
欲	翌	乱	卵	覧	裏	律	臨	朗	論	(190 characters)									

The Kana Systems: *Hiragana* and *Katakana*

The *Hiragana* a-i-u-e-o Arrangement

あ a	か ka	さ sa	た ta	な na	は ha	ま ma	や ya	ら ra	わ wa
い i	き ki	し shi	ち chi	に ni	ひ hi	み mi	い (y)i	り ri	ゐ (w)i
う u	く ku	す su	つ tsu	ぬ nu	ふ fu	む mu	ゆ yu	る ru	う (w)u
え e	け ke	せ se	て te	ね ne	へ he	め me	え (y)e	れ re	ゑ (w)e
お o	こ ko	そ so	と to	の no	ほ ho	も mo	よ yo	ろ ro	を (w)o	ん n

The *Katakana* a-i-u-e-o Arrangement

ア *a*	カ *ka*	サ *sa*	タ *ta*	ナ *na*	ハ *ha*	マ *ma*	ヤ *ya*	ラ *ra*	ワ *wa*	
イ *i*	キ *ki*	シ *shi*	チ *chi*	ニ *ni*	ヒ *hi*	ミ *mi*	イ *(y)i*	リ *ri*	ヰ *(w)i*	
ウ *u*	ク *ku*	ス *su*	ツ *tsu*	ヌ *nu*	フ *fu*	ム *mu*	ユ *yu*	ル *ru*	ウ *(w)u*	
エ *e*	ケ *ke*	セ *se*	テ *te*	ネ *ne*	ヘ *he*	メ *me*	エ *(y)e*	レ *re*	ヱ *(w)e*	
オ *o*	コ *ko*	ソ *so*	ト *to*	ノ *no*	ホ *ho*	モ *mo*	ヨ *yo*	ロ *ro*	ヲ *(w)o*	ン *n*

Appendix D
Japanese Holidays, Ceremonies, and Festivals

January 1—*O-Shōgatsu*/New Year's Day (National Holiday)

Together with the year-end activities in the last days of December, this holiday puts the past behind and marks a new beginning for everyone. Although the official holiday is only one day, most families and businesses observe three days of rest. During this time many people visit relatives, pray at shrines and temples for good fortune in the coming year, and enjoy special New Year's meals and activities.

Traditionally, children fly decorative kites, play with spinning tops, and bat a feathered "birdie" with painted battledores. A New Year's card game containing names of ancient poets and phrases of their poems is enjoyed by young and old; it is a vehicle by which children learn bits of classical literature. Families also bring out the bamboo brush at this time to write New Year's greeting cards to acquaintances and to practice the artistic writing of calligraphy and poetry.

January 15—*Seijin no Hi*/Adult's Day (National Holiday)

This national holiday is dedicated to honoring all twenty-year-olds. The right to vote and to drink alcohol and legal status as an adult are awarded to all those who have reached the age of twenty during the prior year. City halls hold civic ceremonies, and some twenty-year-olds visit shrines on this day. Many of the young women honorees wear kimonos.

February 3 or 4—*Setsubun*/Bean-Throwing Ceremony

To protect their homes against possible harm, people scatter roasted beans at the doors of their homes shouting *Oni wa soto* (Out with the devils!) and *Fuku wa uchi* (In with good fortune!). Teams of children wearing devil masks visit homes in their neighborhood for bean-throwing.

February 11—*Kenkoku Kinen no Hi*/National Founding Day (National Holiday)

March 3—*Hina Matsuri*/Girls' Day

Hina dolls representing imperial court figures are arranged on tiered shelves at home and in some public places for the two weeks prior to this festival for little girls. Traditional sweets are enjoyed in front of the dolls on March 3.

March 20—*Shunbun no Hi*/Vernal Equinox Day (National Holiday)

Mid-April—*O-Hanami*/Cherry Blossom Viewing

When the cherry blossoms break into bloom, signaling the end of winter, groups of schoolchildren, office workers, and families head for public parks to picnic on the grass under the branches of the cherry trees.

April 29—*Tennō Tanjōbi*/The Emperor's Birthday (National Holiday)

This holiday and the next two holidays occur all in one week, which has become known as Golden Week. Many families vacation and travel during this string of holidays.

May 3—*Konpō Kinembi*/Constitution Memorial Day (National Holiday)

May 5—*Kodomo no Hi*/Children's Day (National Holiday)

This day originally was called Boys' Day, the counterpart of Girls' Day on March 3. But when one was chosen to be a national holiday, it became known as Children's Day. Still, the emphasis on May 5 is on the boys. Carp streamers are strung above homes that have young sons, with the hope that they will grow up strong and steady like the carp swimming against the stream. Miniature models of samurai helmets and armor are displayed inside the house.

July 7 or August 7—*Tanabata*/Star Festival

The date of this festival is different in Japan according to region. This is the only day that two stars, Vega and Altair, appear on the same side of the Milky Way. A Chinese legend explains this event with a story of two lovers who can meet only once a year. Children write their wishes on strips of paper and make other paper decorations to hang on a bamboo branch outside the front door.

Mid-July or Mid-August—*O-Bon*/All Souls' Festival

The date of this festival also varies regionally, but all towns in Japan celebrate *O-Bon*. In a three-day period, souls of departed ancestors come back to visit their homes. People who now live in the cities away from their hometowns often return to their native places to help clean the family graves and make special prayers and offerings to the ancestors. In addition to the solemn activities, folk dancing and drumming continue for several nights in the lantern-filled town square.

Many Buddhist churches in California hold a summer festival during *O-Bon*, when everyone is welcome to enjoy Japanese foods, music, dancing, and cultural displays.

September 15—*Keirō no Hi*/Respect for the Aged Day (National Holiday)

September 23—*Shubun no Hi*/Autumnal Equinox Day (National Holiday)

October 10—*Taiiku no Hi*/Health-Sports Day (National Holiday)

Schools hold a field day for all kinds of athletic competitions.

November 3—*Bunka no Hi*/Culture Day (National Holiday)

Schools hold a cultural open house around this time. Elementary school students show off their class projects. In junior and senior high schools, members of youth clubs demonstrate their specialities. Martial arts clubs demonstrate *karate, judo,* or *kendo*. Members of the calligraphy club, the painting club, and the flower arranging club exhibit their work.

November 15—*Shichi-Go-San*/Seven-Five-Three

Girls aged seven to three and boys aged five dress up in kimonos and go to visit a shrine for a blessing, together with their parents or grandparents.

November 23—*Kinro Kansha no Hi*/Labor Thanksgiving Day (National Holiday)

December 25—*Kurisumasu*/Christmas

Christmas is not a traditional holiday in Japan; it is a normal working day and school day. But under the encouragement of merchants and confectioners, children sometimes now exchange small presents and ask their parents to bring home a decorated Christmas cake from the bakery. Some shop owners decorate their shops with plastic Christmas trees and Santa Claus faces in December.

December 31—*Joya no Kane*/Ringing in the New Year

During the last several days of December, people rush around to finish all their business, pay all outstanding debts, clean out needless things that have piled up in the past year, and prepare food and drink for the three days of New Year's feasting. This flurry of activity ends late in the evening on December 31. People all over Japan watch a popular singing competition on television and eat special long noodles, as midnight approaches, to tie together the old and new years. At midnight, the bells at every temple in Japan begin to ring. The bells toll 108 times to clear away all the imperfections of the past year and ring in a fresh start with the new year. People listen solemnly to the bells, and some go out at midnight to make the first prayers of the new year at a nearby temple.

Publications Available from the Department of Education

This publication is one of over 650 that are available from the California State Department of Education. Some of the more recent publications or those most widely used are the following:

ISBN	Title (Date of publication)	Price
0-8011-0271-5	Academic Honesty (1986)	$2.50
0-8011-0471-8	Addendum to the 1985-86 California Private School Directory (1986)	7.75
0-8011-0272-3	Administration of Maintenance and Operations in California School Districts (1986)	6.75
0-8011-0216-2	Bilingual-Crosscultural Teacher Aides: A Resource Guide (1984)	3.50
0-8011-0238-3	Boating the Right Way (1985)	4.00
0-8011-0275-8	California Dropouts: A Status Report (1986)	2.50
0-8011-0472-6	California Private School Directory (1986)	9.00
0-8011-0473-4	California Public School Directory (1987)	14.00
0-8011-0488-2	Caught in the Middle: Educational Reform for Young Adolescents in California Public Schools (1987)	5.00
0-8011-0493-9	Challenge of Excellence: Annual Report, 1986 (1987)	3.00
0-8011-0241-3	Computer Applications Planning (1985)	5.00
0-8011-0242-1	Computers in Education: Goals and Content (1985)	2.50
0-8011-0659-1	Educational Software Preview Guide (1987)	2.00
0-8011-0489-0	Effective Practices in Achieving Compensatory Education-Funded Schools II (1987)	5.00
0-8011-0243-X	Elementary School Program Quality Criteria (1985)	3.25
0-8011-0041-0	English-Language Arts Framework for California Public Schools (1987)	3.00
0-8011-0663-X	English-Language Arts Model Curriculum Guide, K—8 (1987)	2.25
0-8011-0247-2	Handbook for Conducting an Elementary Program Review (1985)	4.50
0-8011-0248-0	Handbook for Conducting a Secondary Program Review (1985)	4.50
0-8011-0289-8	Handbook for Physical Education (1986)	4.50
0-8011-0249-9	Handbook for Planning an Effective Foreign Language Program (1985)	3.50
0-8011-0320-7	Handbook for Planning an Effective Literature Program (1987)	3.00
0-8011-0179-4	Handbook for Planning an Effective Mathematics Program (1982)	2.00
0-8011-0290-1	Handbook for Planning an Effective Writing Program (1986)	2.50
0-8011-0224-3	Handbook for Teaching Cantonese-Speaking Students (1984)	4.50
0-8011-0680-X	Handbook for Teaching Japanese-Speaking Students (1987)	4.50
0-8011-0291-X	Handbook for Teaching Pilipino-Speaking Students (1986)	4.50
0-8011-0204-9	Handbook for Teaching Portuguese-Speaking Students (1983)	4.50
0-8011-0250-2	Handbook on California Education for Language Minority Parents—Chinese/English Edition (1985)	3.25*
0-8011-0227-8	Individual Learning Programs for Limited-English-Proficient Students (1984)	3.50

*The following editions are also available, at the same price: Armenian/English, Cambodian/English, Hmong/English, Korean/English, Laotian/English, Spanish/English, and Vietnamese/English.

0-8011-0466-1	Instructional Patterns: Curriculum for Parenthood Education (1985)	12.00
0-8011-0208-1	Manual of First-Aid Practices for School Bus Drivers (1983)	1.75
0-8011-0209-X	Martin Luther King, Jr., 1929—1968 (1983)	3.25
0-8011-0255-3	Nutrition Education—Compute Well, Be Well: Computer Activities for the Classroom, Preschool/Kindergarten (1985)	12.50
0-8011-0256-1	Nutrition Education—Compute Well, Be Well: Computer Activities for the Classroom, Grades 1—3 (1985)	12.50
0-8011-0257-X	Nutrition Education—Compute Well, Be Well: Computer Activities for the Classroom, Grades 4—6 (1985)	12.50
0-8011-0303-7	A Parent's Handbook on California Education (1986)	3.25
0-8011-0305-3	Paths Through High School: A California Curriculum Study (1987)	4.00
0-8011-0671-0	Practical Ideas for Teaching Writing as a Process (1987)	6.00
0-8011-0309-6	Program Guidelines for Hearing Impaired Individuals (1986)	6.00
0-8011-0258-8	Program Guidelines for Severely Orthopedically Impaired Individuals (1985)	6.00
0-8011-0310-X	Program Guidelines for Visually Impaired Individuals (1986)	6.00
0-8011-0213-8	Raising Expectations: Model Graduation Requirements (1983)	2.75
0-8011-0311-8	Recommended Readings in Literature, K—8 (1986)	2.25
0-8011-0214-6	School Attendance Improvement: A Blueprint for Action (1983)	2.75
0-8011-0189-1	Science Education for the 1980s (1982)	2.50
0-8011-0339-8	Science Framework for California Public Schools (1978)	3.00
0-8011-0354-1	Science Framework Addendum (1984)	3.00
0-8011-0665-6	Science Model Curriculum Guide, K—8 (1987)	3.25
0-8011-0262-6	Secondary School Program Quality Criteria (1985)	3.25
0-8011-0677-X	Secondary Textbook Review: General Mathematics (1987)	6.50
0-8011-0315-0	Selected Financial and Related Data for California Public Schools (1986)	3.00
0-8011-0265-0	Standards for Scoliosis Screening in California Public Schools (1985)	2.50
0-8011-0486-6	Statement on Preparation in Natural Science Expected of Entering Freshmen (1986)	2.50
0-8011-0318-5	Students' Rights and Responsibilities Handbook (1986)	2.75
0-8011-0234-0	Studies on Immersion Education: A Collection for U.S. Educators (1984)	5.00
0-8011-0474-2	Technology in the Curriculum (5 manuals, 5 diskettes) (1986)	95.00
0-8011-0192-1	Trash Monster Environmental Education Kit (for grade six)	23.00
0-8011-0236-7	University and College Opportunities Handbook (1984)	3.25

Orders should be directed to:

California State Department of Education
P.O. Box 271
Sacramento, CA 95802-0271

Please include the International Standard Book Number (ISBN) for each title ordered.

Remittance or purchase order must accompany order. Purchase orders without checks are accepted only from governmental agencies in California. Sales tax should be added to all orders from California purchasers.

A complete list of publications available from the Department, including apprenticeship instructional materials, may be obtained by writing to the address listed above.

84 77344   82-153 03-0490 300 6-87 4,500